KUMIHIMO
WIREWORK

MADE EASY

20 BRAIDED JEWELRY DESIGNS STEP-BY-STEP

CHRISTINA LARSEN

 Interweave

DEDICATION

To Ronnie O'Sullivan, Liang Wenbo, Neil Robertston, and all the other players who played snooker on TV for me to watch while making this book.

Editorial Director | Kerry Bogert

Editor | Jodi Butler

Technical Editor | Cassie Donlen

Art Director &
Cover Designer | Ashlee Wadeson

Interior Designer | Pam Uhlenkamp

Beauty Photographer | David Baum

Step Photographer | George Boe

www.fwcommunity.com

www.interweave.com

22 21 20 19 18   5 4 3 2 1

E-mail: enquiries@fwmedia.com

SRN: 18JM02

ISBN-13: 978-1-63250-635-1

CONTENTS

INTRODUCTION

Kumihimo is an ancient Japanese braiding technique originally used with fiber, which is still the most common material. As the art form has evolved and gained recent popularity, a variety of materials have been introduced into this fascinating technique. Using wire in place of fiber offers new design possibilities as wire responds differently than fiber when braided. A simple act such as removing your braid from the disk without
having to worry about it unraveling is possible because unlike fiber, wire holds its shape.

This feature offers new opportunities for what can be done in the world of kumihimo. Braiding wire also leads to a very different finish and appearance of the final piece. Many of the designs in this book explore a variety of ideas for using wire when making braids. I've discovered that experimenting with alternate design ideas that pop into my mind while braiding a particular piece is the best way to evolve and invent fresh beautiful designs.

Before starting any projects, I highly recommend reading the beginning sections of this book thoroughly as there is a bit of a learning curve with wire kumihimo. Also, try practicing the basic braid structures with less expensive wire or cord until you are comfortable with the techniques. Once you are ready to start the projects, you can refer back to the beginning tutorials as needed.

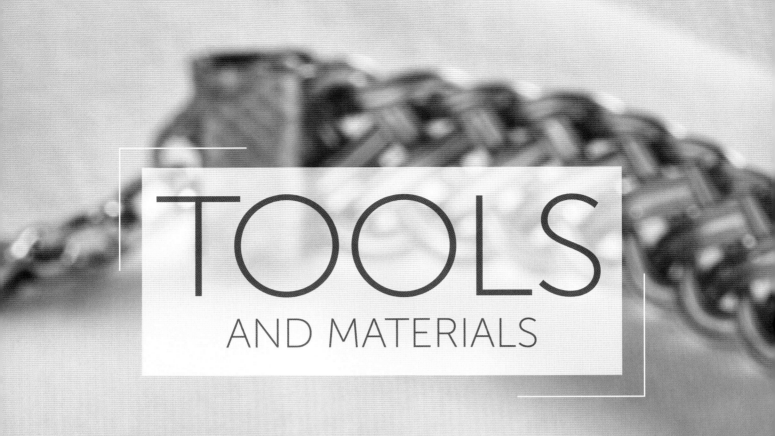

TOOLS
AND MATERIALS

Choosing the right materials and tools for wire kumihimo is important as they can greatly impact the outcome. Sometimes specific materials or tools are needed to achieve a particular design, while other times you can branch out and experiment with alternatives. I detail the most important things to keep in mind when choosing the materials and tools to use for your wire kumihimo jewelry in this section.

WIRE 101

There are several things to take into consideration when choosing materials for wire kumihimo jewelry: what kind of wire to use, which beads fit within the design, and how to finish pieces. Some designs require specific materials to form the braid properly, while others can be customized to work with different materials, depending on the desired look. Choosing a bead with an alternate shape to the one featured in the book could work, but it may give the finished piece a different look. It all comes down to personal preference. Feel free to choose different materials than those featured in the projects, and have fun experimenting!

WIRE HARDNESS

You can use different types of wire for kumihimo. I recommend using a softer wire, such as bare copper, plated copper, craft wire, or sterling silver, because it makes the working process easier and tends to result in a tighter, more even braid. The finished braids are also easier to shape, if the design calls for it.

For wire that has different hardnesses available (see Wire Hardness Explained), I recommend using the dead-soft hardness for the reasons previously stated. Usually the concern with using soft wire is that it won't hold the desired shape as well as harder wire, but that is not as much of a concern with wire kumihimo. There are a few reasons for this. First, there are multiple wires being used at the same time for each braid, which adds to the

strength of the final piece, as opposed to jewelry that is made using only one length of wire. Second, as the wire is manipulated it work hardens (becomes stiffer), which in turn makes it stronger. This is beneficial when using wire to make kumihimo because the many movements of forming the braid with the soft wire will result in a strong final piece of jewelry, while still using wire that is easy to work with.

WIRE GAUGE

Wire is widely available in several thicknesses, which are referred to as the *wire gauge*. The larger the gauge number, the thinner the wire. I recommend using 20–30-gauge wire for kumihimo designs as thicker wire is difficult to work with and harder on your hands.

BUYING WIRE

Wire kumihimo tends to use a fair amount of wire due to the nature of the braiding. Wire comes in both small coils and large reels, so it is important to pay attention to the amount of wire required when gathering supplies. I've eliminated the guesswork by including the exact amount needed to complete each project in the materials list.

This Elegant Bracelet features twisted wire, which emphasizes the braid structure.

WIRE HARDNESS EXPLAINED

When making jewelry with wire, you will often see or hear the term *wire hardness*. This indicates how much resistance the wire has when bending it. There are usually three different wire hardnesses: dead soft (soft), half hard, and full hard. These all have their place and present different characteristics when working with them. Dead-soft wire is easy to work with but not ideal to use by itself without work hardening it, whereas full-hard wire is very stiff and more difficult to work with but will be much stronger and hold its shape better. Half-hard wire falls in between these two and can be considered the best of both worlds. When working with heavier gauge wires, dead-soft wire and half-hard wire are also more prone to needing work hardening to make them stronger, whereas full-hard wire is often already strong enough.

BEADS FOR KUMIHIMO

Deciding on the type of beads to use for wire kumihimo jewelry is a personal decision and depends on how you want the final piece to look. Some designs will work with many different beads, so you can choose from a variety of types, shapes, and sizes, depending on the look you want. Other designs require beads in specific shapes or sizes to achieve the desired effect.

The most important thing to look for when choosing beads is the size of the holes because they need to be large enough to fit over the wire used to make the braid. It can sometimes be a problem if the holes in your chosen beads are too small for the wire to go through. To avoid disappointment, make sure the wire fits inside each bead hole before starting your project.

There are certain types of beads that work well with wire kumihimo. So, delve into the world of beads and cabochons, and find your personal favorites.

GLASS BEADS

ROSE MONTÉES

SEED BEADS

CABOCHON

METAL SPACER BEADS

SEED BEADS

Seed beads are an obvious choice because they come in a vast array of colors and shapes, and their holes tend to be fairly large for incorporating thin gauge wire, including the smaller size seed beads. Just be mindful that seed beads are made of glass and can break if too much pressure is exerted on them.

Other glass beads, such as Czech or crystal beads, work well and are available in round and bicone shapes, but like seed beads are slightly fragile. Rose montées are made with crystal rhinestones but have a metal backing that makes them stronger. They also feature multiple holes on the metal back, which offer additional design possibilities.

METAL SPACER BEADS

Metal spacer beads are a good option because they are strong and the holes tend to be generous, but the choices in colors and shapes can be limited.

GEMSTONES

Gemstone beads are a wonderful choice and my personal favorite because there are so many options for color, size, and shape. Plus, there can also be a more personal connection with certain gemstones. The downside is that they tend to have smaller holes and can be difficult to drill. I have found a few types of gemstones that work well for wire kumihimo because they often have larger holes, even in small bead sizes, and are also very strong. These include hematite, agate, and quartz; thankfully the shapes and colors in these stones are vast. I also love to use gemstone cabochons because there are so many types, shapes, and colors to choose from. They also tend to be very strong and are therefore perfect for surrounding with wire kumihimo.

CHOOSING THE RIGHT LEATHER

Using different materials in the same design can change the look of the final piece. Incorporating leather into wire kumihimo designs can add more color and also bring in a different texture, which may alter a design completely. It is easy to incorporate round leather into wire kumihimo because it is similar to cord, and mixing the two is like combining the best of both worlds. You get the strength and elegance of wire plus the softness and texture of leather.

I recommend using good quality, soft leather because it is durable and blends well with wire. You can also mold it around the shape of the wire more easily than harder leather, which will give the braid a neater finish. Leather comes in a variety of thicknesses, so check the project directions for advice on which leather to use.

ROUND
LEATHER

FINISHING COMPONENTS

LARGE RIBBON END

SMALL RIBBON END

RIBBON ENDS

Finishing the ends of your wire kumihimo is a simple but important step. A properly finished end will prevent the wires from unraveling, conceal the cut ends, and provide a secure way to attach a clasp to the piece. When finished properly, the wire ends won't catch on clothing or scratch your skin when being worn. I like to use ribbon-end components to finish many of my wire kumihimo pieces, especially bracelets, because they are flat and match the wire ends perfectly. This provides a neat, professional-looking finish, and lets you attach a clasp of your choice directly onto the loop of the ribbon end.

Ribbon ends come in many different sizes and finishes, making it easy to match the ribbon ends perfectly to the braid's width. To choose the correct size ribbon end, simply measure the width of the finished braid and match that to the width of the ribbon end.

FINDINGS

Choosing findings for your projects is a personal preference. In most cases, the findings are attached to the loops on the ribbon-end components. I like to use two jump rings to attach a lobster clasp on one end (technically you only need one) and an extender chain on the opposite end. I think this gives the jewelry a professional look and also has the added benefit of making the length adjustable, without taking attention away from the design. But other clasps, such as toggle clasps, can easily be used as well.

Earring findings also come down to personal taste. I normally use earring posts and butterfly backs, but you can just as easily attach earrings to the findings of your choice, such as ear wire hooks.

Head pins are another finding that is used in several projects in the book. Different types of head pins are available, but they all perform the same function. With flat head pins, the end that traps the bead is flat and is almost invisible. Ball-end head pins are intended to be more decorative and feature a round tiny ball on the tip that stays visible and becomes part of the design. Head pins are also available in several lengths. The extra length can be useful if you are using larger beads that require additional wire when wire wrapping.

EARRING FINDINGS

JUMP RINGS

LOBSTER CLAW CLASPS

TOOLS

You only need a few basic tools to make wire kumihimo jewelry: A kumihimo disk, wire cutters, and two basic pliers for handling the wire and attaching findings. A few extra tools are also recommended, but they are not crucial as many of them are interchangeable with other tools or household items.

THE KUMIHIMO DISK

The most important tool for wire kumihimo is the disk, which you need to create braids for the different designs. The kumihimo disk is an inexpensive round or square shaped foam board with evenly placed slots around the sides and a hole in the center, where the braid is formed. The slots are used to hold the wires while they are being moved in different patterns to achieve the different braid structures. These slots will become loose fairly quickly when using wire as kumihimo. Fortunately, it isn't crucial for the slots to stay tight when using wire as it is when using cord. (Unlike cord, the slots are primarily used for holding the wires in place rather than helping with the tension.) For all of the designs in this book, we are using the square kumihimo disk, which is primarily used for making flat braids. The number of slots along the edge of the disk can vary depending on the manufacturer. This will not affect the braid, but make sure to always work in the middle slots on each side when creating the braids.

> **TIP**
>
> IF THE SLOT IDENTIFICATION MARKERS ON YOUR DISK DO NOT CORRELATE WITH THE DISK REFERENCED IN THE BOOK, SIMPLY FLIP YOUR DISK OVER TO THE BLANK SIDE. USING A PERMANENT MARKER, WRITE THE SLOT NUMBERS AND LETTERS IN A CORRESPONDING PATTERN. USE THE HANDWRITTEN SIDE AS THE FRONT OF THE KUMIHIMO DISK.

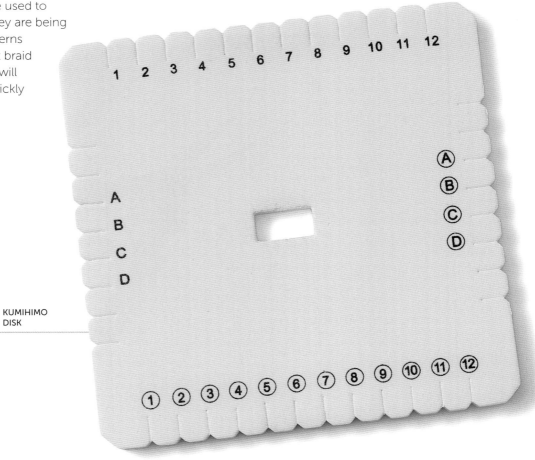

KUMIHIMO DISK

WIRE CUTTERS AND PLIERS

Wire cutters perform the essential task of cutting and trimming wire. Additionally, two different pairs of pliers are also needed to help manipulate and grasp the wire and attach the findings.

WIRE CUTTERS | Wire cutters are the perfect tool for cutting the long lengths of wire used to make the braids. I recommend flush cutters for designs that do not use ribbon ends because they provide a cleaner cut than standard wire cutters, which can help prevent wire burrs that can catch on clothes or scratch skin and will also give a cleaner finish to the jewelry. Since the projects in this book use fine gauge wire, it isn't necessary to have heavy-duty wire cutters that cut up to 12-gauge thick wire. Basic wire cutters will be perfect for the job.

PLIERS | Either flat-nose or chain-nose pliers can be used for bending wire and gaining a better grip on wire than your fingers alone. The chain-nose plier's pointed tips are especially useful for tucking away wire ends as they can reach into smaller spaces than flat-nose pliers. But both flat-nose and chain-nose pliers will be needed when using jump rings to attach findings. Nylon-jaw pliers are useful for straightening and hardening wire. They also protect delicate wire from scratches and marring.

FINE ROUND-NOSE PLIERS | Keep a pair of round-nose pliers handy for when you need to make loops or widen the gaps within a braid.

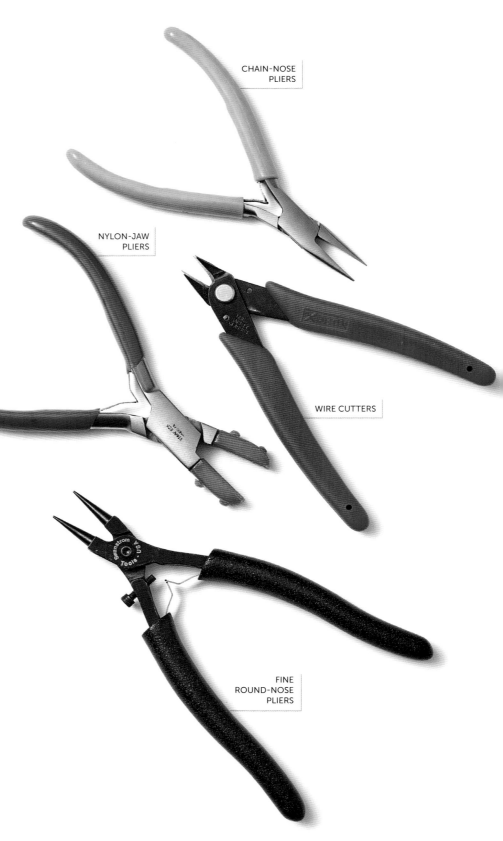

CHAIN-NOSE PLIERS

NYLON-JAW PLIERS

WIRE CUTTERS

FINE ROUND-NOSE PLIERS

GENERAL TOOLS AND SUPPLIES

In addition to basic pliers and wire cutters, you will need the following items to properly complete your projects.

TAPE | Tape is crucial for making wire kumihimo. It is used for making every braid in this book because it gives a starting point and helps keep the wires under control while braiding. I recommend using black electrical insulation tape. It is strong and easy to use, without being too sticky. Keep the tape on the wires during the entire braiding process, then remove it when you're done. If any excess residue from the tape remains on the wires, it can easily be removed by running the wire through your fingers a few times.

GLUE | Adhesive is essential for jewelry making. It can help add extra strength and durability to your pieces, but it is important to find the right kind of glue. When working with wire, use glue that is compatible with metal, has a strong hold, and dries clear. That way if you're adding ribbon ends and the glue seeps out a little, it isn't too obvious. My favorite glue is E6000 adhesive because it doesn't dry too quickly and is easy to apply with a toothpick. It has a strong odor though, so it is recommended to use E6000 in a well-ventilated area. Let the glue cure for 24 hours before wearing the jewelry.

RING AND BRACELET MANDRELS | Mandrels are needed for sizing and shaping jewelry. Most mandrels are made of metal, but ring mandrels can often be found in the more economical plastic version. You will need a ring mandrel for making wire kumihimo rings. A bracelet mandrel is also required, but it can be more easily replaced

JEWELER'S GLUE

by household items of a similar size and shape, such as cups or containers. Some designs use different size mandrels to help make one piece. For that reason, I recommend using multi-step mandrels that offer different sizes within one tool.

There are two small mandrels that I find particularly handy. One mandrel covers five sizes from 1.5–5 mm in diameter, while the other covers five sizes from 6–10 mm. These mandrels help when shaping braids and can also be used for making loops. I recommend having a plastic multi-mandrel available for shaping some of the braids. It is inexpensive and offers multiple shapes in different sizes. If you don't have any of these mandrels available, you can often improvise with household items. So have a look around your home, and see what you have that might work for the project you want to make.

MEASURING TAPE | A measuring tape is crucial for wire kumihimo. You will use it for measuring the wire needed for making braids and for measuring braids as you make them to ensure they are the proper length for the project. You will also need a measuring tape for finishing off bracelets when attaching ribbon ends, so you can cut the braids to the proper length. Any type of measuring tape or ruler will work, but when measuring long lengths of wire, it is beneficial to use a longer measuring tape to be able to measure it in a single length.

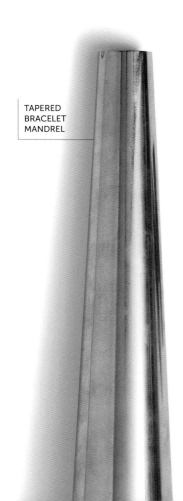

TAPERED BRACELET MANDREL

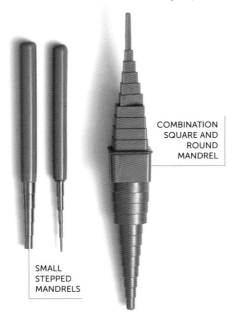

SMALL STEPPED MANDRELS

COMBINATION SQUARE AND ROUND MANDREL

BASIC
TECHNIQUES

This is probably the most important section of the book because it covers the basic techniques for making wire kumihimo jewelry. It is important to understand how to prepare and move wires around a kumihimo board before learning the braid structures. You will also learn how to use wire for kumihimo to achieve the finished results, as there is a bit of a learning curve. Once you have the basics in place, you can comfortably move on to the projects, and also start to experiment with your own designs.

PREPARING WIRES FOR BRAIDING

Before beginning a braid, you need to prepare the lengths of wire to make them as easy to work with as possible. This involves straightening, securing, and in some cases, twisting the wires. Some designs also call for leaving both ends of the braid temporarily unfinished so additional steps can be completed to achieve the final design. Here, you will learn how to set up your wire to achieve this.

STRAIGHTENING WIRE

Before cutting wire for a project, it needs to be straightened to avoid kinks or bends, which can weaken the wire and affect the look of the final braid. Here are several ways to straighten wire.

> **NOTE** | FOR EACH METHOD, I RECOMMEND STRAIGHTENING WIRE WHILE IT IS STILL ATTACHED TO THE SPOOL. IT IS MUCH EASIER TO GRASP THE SPOOL WHILE STRAIGHTENING THE WIRE THAN HOLDING SHORT LENGTHS OF WIRE IN YOUR HAND.

FINGERS | Simply pinch the wire and run your fingers along the length of the wire several times, while working against the existing curve to even it out. This process also warms up the wire, making it easier to straighten and manipulate. I like using this technique.

NYLON-JAW PLIERS | Following the same principle as the previous method, work against the existing curve in the wire to even it out using a pair of nylon-jaw pliers instead of your fingers **(FIGURE 1)**. Nylon-jaw pliers are especially useful for lengths of wire that are tough to straighten as you can get a better grip on the wire.

WIRE-STRAIGHTENING TOOL | A wire-straightening tool wraps around the length of wire, then the wire is pulled through the tool to straighten it **(FIGURE 2)**.

FIG | 1

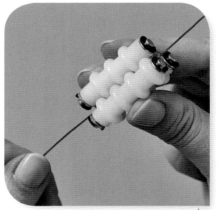

FIG | 2

TIP
WORKING WITH WIRE FOR KUMIHIMO CAN BE TOUGH ON YOUR HANDS AND FINGERS, SO TAKE BREAKS. BECAUSE WIRE HOLDS ITS SHAPE, YOU CAN EASILY PUT YOUR WORK-IN-PROGRESS DOWN WITHOUT WORRYING ABOUT IT GETTING RUINED.

FIG | 3

SECURING WIRE

After you cut all of the wire for a project, lay the pieces flat next to each other with the ends evenly lined up. Cut a 1½–2" (3.8–5 cm) piece of electrical tape and place it near one end of the wires, making sure to leave a short length of wires sticking out underneath the tape, about ¼" (6 mm) **(FIGURE 3)**. If the project calls for starting further up the wire, place the tape where specified. Wrap the tape tightly around the wires, making sure the lengths stay flat next to one another.

NOTE | FOR PROJECTS USING RIBBON ENDS, IT CAN BE BENEFICIAL TO BEND BACK THE VERY TIPS OF THE WIRE THAT ARE STICKING OUT FROM UNDER THE TAPE **(FIGURE 4)**. THIS WILL PREVENT THE WIRES FROM BEING PULLED OUT OF THE TAPE WHEN STARTING TO MAKE THE BRAID.

FIG | 4

TIP

IT'S EASIER TO GET A GRIP ON THE BRAID AND MORE PRECISE BENDING BY USING A PAIR OF CHAIN-NOSE PLIERS INSTEAD OF YOUR FINGERS.

TWISTED WIRE

Some designs use twisted wire to achieve a different effect. You can buy twisted wire or twist regular round wire yourself. There are several wire-twisting tools available on the market or you can use a drill. Whichever method you use, it's important to note the length of the original wires being twisted will get reduced by about 10 percent for the final length of twisted wire. Keep this in mind when cutting lengths of wire to twist, depending on what lengths are required for use in the design.

When twisting wire, I recommend cutting one long length of wire and folding it in half before twisting rather than twisting two separate wires. This will waste less wire and also leave a loop in one end, which can be securely attached around something, such as a door handle, to start twisting from. The two open ends of the wire can then be attached to either a wire-twisting tool or a drill to start twisting them together. Twist the wire until it reaches the tightness you prefer, but be careful not to overtwist it or the wire can break. When you're done, just slide the wire off the doorknob and cut off the loop on one end and the bent wire on the other before using in the braid.

USING WIRE FOR KUMIHIMO

Working with wire for kumihimo is different than using fiber. It requires some practice to get comfortable with the techniques and achieve the desired results. I recommend practicing with less expensive wire while you're getting used to working with wire and learning how to make the basic braids.

HOLDING THE WIRE

Once you have prepared the wires for braiding (see Preparing Wires for Braiding), attach them to the kumihimo disk by putting the taped end front to back through the center hole in the disk and placing the working lengths of wire in the slots according to the braid structure instructions. Hold the wires at the taped end tightly with your fingers as close to the underside of the disk as possible while braiding **(FIGURE 1)**. Then keep moving your hand up the braid as you go so it stays under the disk to give you the most control **(FIGURE 2)**.

Sometimes a braid might come out a little misshapen underneath the disk **(FIGURE 3)**. Simply straighten it as you go, so you end up with a straight braid **(FIGURE 4)**.

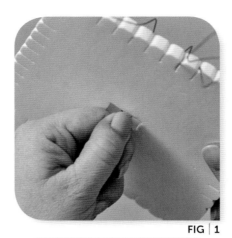

FIG | 1

FIG | 2

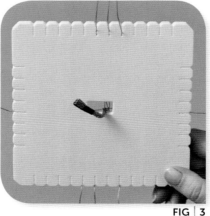

FIG | 3

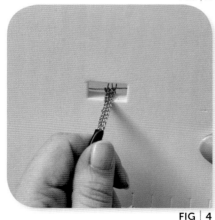

FIG | 4

> ## TIP
> WHEN MAKING THE BRAID, HOLD THE OPEN END OF THE BRAID AGAINST THE BACK OF THE HOLE IN THE CENTER OF THE DISK.

BRAID TENSION

When making kumihimo braids with wire, achieving the right tension in the braid is important. If the tension is too loose, the braid will become unmanageable and you won't achieve the desired results. The goal is to get the different lengths of wire to lay as close to each other as possible within the braid. This creates a firm braid structure that can still be shaped, and you can still fit a length of wire of the same gauge through the gaps between the wires within the braid. Practice the tension of the braids, until you feel comfortable and find your own rhythm, by following the 'Moving your wires' section.

MOVING THE WIRE

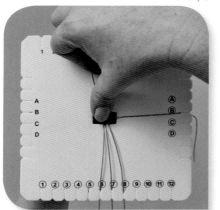

FIG | 5

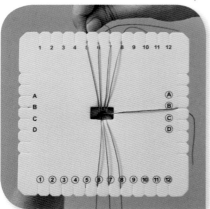

FIG | 6

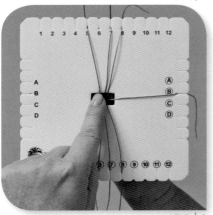

FIG | 7

It is important to remember that wire responds differently than fiber. Fiber cord is soft and easy to move, so it is easier to achieve a tighter and more even braid structure. Wire, on the other hand, is a hard material and not as easy to move as cord, so you can't achieve a completely tight braid structure with wire. But you can achieve a fairly tight and even braid structure by working with the wires in specific ways when moving them on the disk. (This is the same principle for all the braid structures.)

When moving wires from the top or bottom of the disk to the sides, pull the wire with a tight tension and press down where the wire is laying across the end of the braid so it sits as close to the other wires as possible **(FIGURE 5)**. Then place the wire in the slot on the side of the disk.

When moving wires from the bottom of the disk to the top, bring the wire up toward the top, while using your thumb to press the wire against the other wires it is crossing over at the end of the braid in a rolling motion **(FIGURE 6)**. Then place the wire in the slot on the top of the disk **(FIGURE 7)**. Use the same principle when bringing a wire from the top to the bottom of the disk, using your index finger **(FIGURE 8)** instead of your thumb to press against the wires at the end of the braid while moving it in a rolling motion.

When you have a wire on the side of the disk that you need to bring back into the braid, use either your index finger or thumb to press against the side of the braid as you are moving the wire to either the bottom or top of the disk. Alternate between using both hands when making these movements with your wire, depending on the braid structure.

TIPS FOR MOVING WIRE

• Every time you move a wire on the disk, run the wire through your fingers before placing it into the next slot. This will help straighten out any bends and kinks in the wire that will appear from using it on the kumihimo disk, and also help prevent damage and breakage to the wire.

• Sometimes lengths of wire that are next to each other will start to overlap on the disk. This is due to the curve that is put into the wire while straightening it and also from pressing against the end of the braid in the middle of the wire. It is normal and has no effect on the final braid as long as you make sure to keep the wires in their correct slots on the disk.

• For projects where you don't bend the ends of the wires poking out from under the taped end, make sure to keep a tight grip on the wires below the disk and avoid pulling too hard when doing the first few movements of the braid to avoid pulling the lengths of wire out of the tape. After a few movements of braiding, the end becomes more secure and you can loosen your grip on the wires under the disk.

FIG | 8

BRAID
STRUCTURES

There are three basic braid structures used for the designs in this book: a Diagonal Kumihimo, a Cross Kumihimo, and a Half-Round Kumihimo. Some projects use only one braid structure, while others use two within the same design. For all the basic braid structures, start by preparing your wires (see Preparing Wires for Braiding). I recommend practicing the basic braid structures using 12" (30.5 cm) lengths of inexpensive wire, such as craft wire or florist wire. This length is more manageable and you can still achieve a decent braid, while finding your rhythm and getting familiar with the tension needed to create braids with wire. If you're just getting started with wire kumihimo, you can also start out practicing braid structures with cord. Then move on to practicing with less expensive wire before starting the projects in this book.

DIAGONAL KUMIHIMO STRUCTURE

This braid got its name from the diagonal look in the finished braid structure. Eight lengths of wire are used to demonstrate the basic braid structure, but the technique can also be used with more or fewer wires. This braid structure is easier for beginners and looks great using the wire by itself. It is also ideal for incorporating beads into the braid to create interesting designs.

NOTE | THESE DIRECTIONS ARE BASED ON A KUMIHIMO DISK WITH 12 NUMBERED SLOTS ON THE TOP AND BOTTOM AND 4 LETTERED SLOTS ON EACH SIDE. SLOT NUMBERS AND LETTERS MAY DIFFER DEPENDING ON THE DISK YOU ARE USING.

> **TIP**
>
> THIS BRAID STRUCTURE IS IDEAL FOR DESIGNS WHERE THE FINAL BRAID NEEDS TO BE SHAPED TO ACHIEVE THE DESIRED LOOK.

1 Cut and straighten eight equal lengths of wire (see Straightening Wire in Basic Techniques). Lay the wires side by side, lining up the ends. Wrap a piece of electrical tape around one end.

2 Insert the taped end though the hole in the disk and hold it tightly just underneath. Working from left to right and using the middle four slots in the top and bottom of the disk, place the first wire in top slot 5, the second wire in bottom slot 5, the third wire in top slot 6, the fourth in bottom slot 6, and so on. Continue alternating the wires until all wires are placed **(FIGURE 1)**.

3 Move the wire from top slot 5 across the center toward the right side of the disk, pressing down in the middle where the wire crosses over the other wires. Place this wire in right slot B **(FIGURE 2)**.

4 Release the wire from bottom slot 5, using your thumb to push against the wires in the middle, and move it to top slot 5 **(FIGURE 3)**.

5 Move the wire from top slot 6 to bottom slot 5, bringing it across the middle of the disk and using your index finger to press against the wires in the middle **(FIGURE 4)**.

6 Move the wire from bottom slot 6 to top slot 6, bringing it across the middle of the disk, while using your thumb to press against the wires in the middle. Continue working in the same manner, using your fingers to position the wire: moving top slot 7 to bottom slot 6, bottom slot 7 to top slot 7, top slot 8 to bottom slot 7, and bottom slot 8 to top slot 8. Now all of the wires on the top and bottom of the disk have moved once **(FIGURE 5)**.

7 To bind the braid, move the wire from right slot B to bottom slot 8, using your index finger to press against the side of the wires in the middle of the disk.

8 The wires have now traveled around the disk and are back in the original setup **(FIGURE 6)**. For Diagonal Kumihimo, this is considered one full round of the technique. To continue the braid, repeat steps 3–7 until the desired length is achieved, and then individually remove each wire from its slot. The finished braid will be flat with two sides. The flatter side is referred to as the front throughout this book and is the side facing toward you while making the braid on the disk. The opposite side is referred to as the back of the braid.

> **NOTE** | IF DESIRED, ALTER THE WIDTH OF THE BRAID BY USING MORE OR LESS THAN EIGHT WIRES. THE EXACT SAME STEPS ARE NEEDED TO FORM THE BRAID. THE ONLY DIFFERENCE IS THE NUMBER OF WIRES BEING MOVED BETWEEN THE TOP AND THE BOTTOM OF THE DISK, WHILE STILL STARTING FROM THE LEFT AND MOVING TOWARD THE RIGHT. REMEMBER TO MOVE THE SINGLE WIRE ON THE SIDE OF THE DISK TO THE EMPTY SLOT ON EITHER THE TOP OR THE BOTTOM, SO THE WIRES END UP IN THEIR ORIGINAL CONFIGURATION. THEN CONTINUE WORKING AS IN STEPS 3–7.

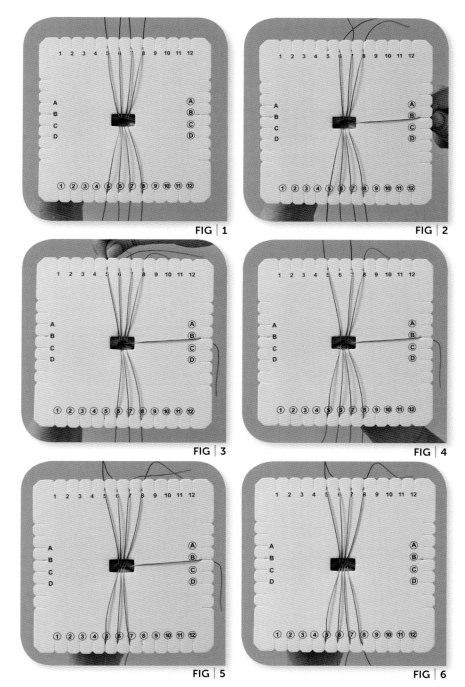

FIG | 1

FIG | 2

FIG | 3

FIG | 4

FIG | 5

FIG | 6

CROSS KUMIHIMO STRUCTURE

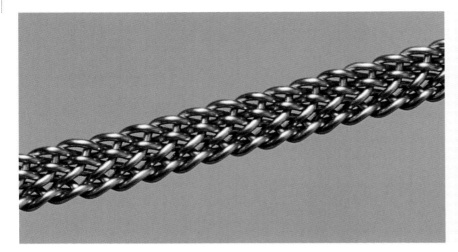

The Cross Kumihimo structure can also be made using more or fewer wires, but it is demonstrated here using eight lengths. It may take a bit of practice to get comfortable with this braid structure and achieve the desired result. For this technique, it is especially important to focus on the Moving the Wire section in Basic Techniques as it greatly affects the final result.

NOTE | THESE DIRECTIONS ARE BASED ON A KUMIHIMO DISK WITH 12 NUMBERED SLOTS ON THE TOP AND BOTTOM AND 4 LETTERED SLOTS ON THE SIDE. SLOT NUMBERS AND LETTERS MAY DIFFER DEPENDING ON THE DISK YOU ARE USING.

TIP

PRACTICE GETTING THE TENSION ON THIS BRAID STRUCTURE TIGHT, AS IT WILL BECOME UNMANAGEABLE IF BRAIDED LOOSELY. REMEMBER TO USE YOUR FINGERS TO PRESS THE TRAVELING WIRE DOWN AGAINST THE BRAID IN THE MIDDLE AS YOU WORK IT.

1 Cut and straighten eight equal lengths of wire (see Straightening Wire in Basic Techniques). Lay the wires side by side, lining up the ends. Wrap a piece of electrical tape around one end.

2 Insert the taped end though the hole in the disk and hold it tightly just underneath. Place the two middle wires in slots 6 and 7 on the bottom of the disk, then place the adjacent wire on each side of these two wires in slots 6 and 7 on the top of the disk **(FIGURE 1)**. Move the adjacent wire on each side of these two wires to slots 5 and 8 on the bottom of the disk and the remaining two outer wires to slots 5 and 8 on the top of the disk **(FIGURE 2)**.

3 Move the wire from top slot 7 to left B slot, and while bringing it into position, use your index finger to press it down against the wires in the middle **(FIGURE 3)**. Repeat this step, moving the wire in top slot 6 to right B slot **(FIGURE 4)**.

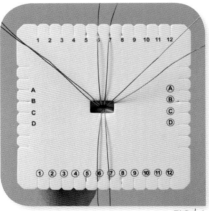

FIG | 1

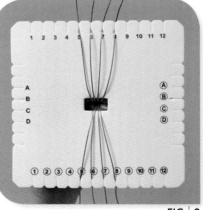

FIG | 2

4 Move the wire from bottom slot 6 to the top slot 6 **(FIGURE 5)**.

5 Move the wire from top slot 5 to bottom slot 6 **(FIGURE 6)**. Move the wire from bottom slot 5 to top slot 5 **(FIGURE 7)**.

6 Working as before, but moving toward the right, move the wire from bottom slot 7 to top slot 7 **(FIGURE 8)**. Move the wire from top slot 8 to bottom slot 7, and bottom slot 8 to top slot 8 **(FIGURE 9)**.

7 To bind the braid, move the wire from left slot B to bottom slot 5, pressing against the side of the wires in the middle while bringing it down. Move the wire from right slot B to bottom slot 8, pressing against the side of the braid in the middle **(FIGURE 10)**.

8 The wires have now swapped places but are back in the original setup. This is considered one full round of the technique. To continue making the braid, repeat steps 3–7 to reach the desired length. When you have completed the braid and removed it from the disk, the two sides of the braid will be slightly different. One side is flatter and considered the front of the braid, which is the side facing you while you are braiding on the disk. The other side is slightly less flat and considered the back of the braid.

NOTE | WHETHER YOU'RE USING MORE OR LESS WIRES FOR THIS BRAID STRUCTURE, REPEAT THE EXACT SAME TECHNIQUE. MAKE THE INITIAL MOVES AS IN STEP 3, AND MAKE SURE THE REMAINING WIRES FOLLOW THE PATTERN IN STEPS 4-6. WHEN BRINGING THE SIDE SLOT B WIRES BACK INTO THE BRAID, BE SURE TO PLACE THEM IN THE EMPTY SLOTS TO REACH THE ORIGINAL STARTING POSITION, WHETHER THAT MEANS BRINGING THEM TO THE TOP OR THE BOTTOM OF THE DISK.

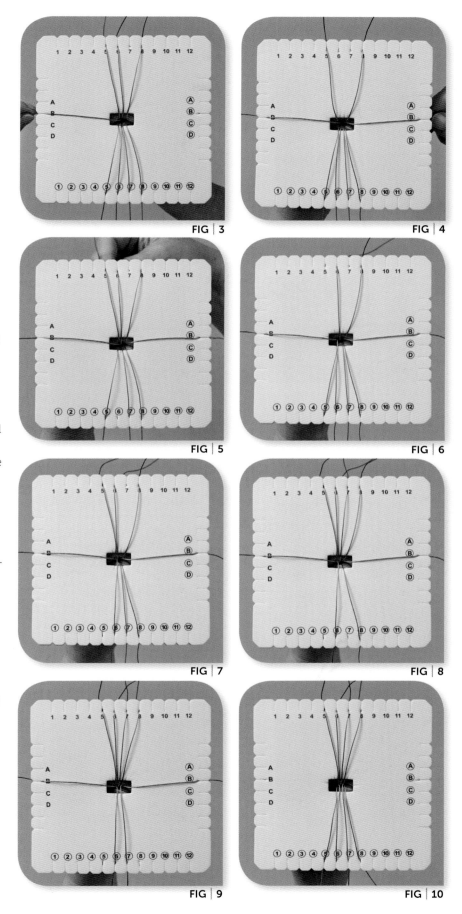

FIG | 3

FIG | 4

FIG | 5

FIG | 6

FIG | 7

FIG | 8

FIG | 9

FIG | 10

HALF-ROUND KUMIHIMO STRUCTURE

When making this braid with fiber, it ends up with one flat side and one slightly rounded side. It doesn't quite have the same effect when using wire as the braid ends up being flatter even though it is the same basic braid structure. Eight lengths of wire are used to demonstrate this braid structure. Additional lengths can be used, but the designs in this book only incorporate eight lengths.

NOTE | THESE DIRECTIONS ARE BASED ON A KUMIHIMO DISK WITH 12 NUMBERED SLOTS ON THE TOP AND BOTTOM AND 4 LETTERED SLOTS ON THE SIDE. SLOT NUMBERS AND LETTERS MAY DIFFER DEPENDING ON THE DISK YOU ARE USING.

1 Cut eight lengths of wire and straighten them (see Straightening Wire in Basic Techniques).
Lay the wires side by side, lining up the ends. Wrap a piece of electrical tape around one end, making sure they lay flat next to each other.

2 Insert the taped end through the hole in the disk and hold it tightly just underneath. Distribute the wires by placing the two middle wires in slots 6 and 7 on the top of the disk, then place the adjacent wire on each side of these wires in slots 6 and 7 on the bottom of the disk. Place the two wires on the far left into slots B and C on the left side of the disk and the remaining two wires on the far right into slots B and C on the right side of the disk **(FIGURE 1)**.

FIG | 1

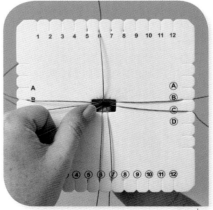

FIG | 2

3 Move the wire in top slot 7 to left slot D, pressing down on top of the wires in the middle with your thumb or index finger as you bring it over to the left side of the disk **(FIGURE 2)**. Move the wire in top slot 6 to right slot D in the same manner **(FIGURE 3)**.

4 Move the wire in bottom slot 7 to left slot A, using your thumb to press against the wires in the middle while moving it to the side **(FIGURE 4)**. Working in the same manner, move the wire in bottom slot 6 to right slot A **(FIGURE 5)**.

5 Move the wire in left slot B to bottom slot 6 **(FIGURE 6)**. Move the wire in left slot C to top slot 6.

6 Repeat the same steps on the right side of the disk, by moving the wire in right slot B to bottom slot 7 **(FIGURE 7)**. Move the wire in right slot C to top slot 7 **(FIGURE 8)**.

7 Close the gaps between the wires on each side of the disk: Move all four wires one slot closer to each other, so they end up in the middle in corresponding slots B and C **(FIGURE 9)**. This completes one full round of the technique and is the original setup all the wires were placed in, except the wires have swapped places.

8 Repeat steps 3–7 to continue building the braid to the desired length. When the braid is finished, remove it from the disk. The braid will have two sides that are slightly different. While you are braiding on the disk, the side that is facing toward you is the front of the braid, and the side that is facing away from you is the back of the braid.

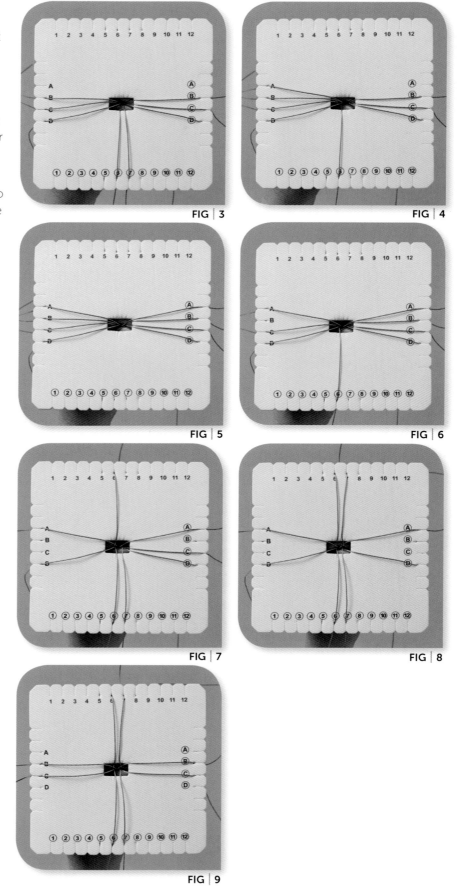

FIG | 3

FIG | 4

FIG | 5

FIG | 6

FIG | 7

FIG | 8

FIG | 9

FINISHING
KUMIHIMO

The braids in this book are
finished in different methods.
In some designs, the ends of
the wires are brought back into
the braid, while others contain
ribbon ends for attaching
clasps that give the braids
a professional-looking finish.

ATTACHING RIBBON ENDS

When you've completed braiding your wire, you're just a few steps of away from finishing your project. While some projects will have you tie the wire ends back into the braid structure, many are finished with ribbon ends.

1 Using wire cutters, cut straight across the braid at the measured point **(FIGURE 1)**.

2 Using a toothpick, add a small amount of E6000 adhesive to the inside of the ribbon end, making sure to coat both sides **(FIGURE 2)**.

> **NOTE** | BE CAREFUL NOT TO ADD TOO MUCH GLUE, OR IT WILL SPILL OUT FROM THE RIBBON END WHEN CLAMPING IT DOWN. ADD THE EXCESS GLUE FROM THE TOOTHPICK TO THE EDGE OF THE CUT BRAID, MAKING SURE IT GETS IN BETWEEN THE WIRES WITHIN THE BRAID.

3 Place the ribbon end on the trimmed end of the braid. Using a pair of flat-nose pliers, clamp down on the ribbon end, making sure the braid stays centered **(FIGURE 3)**. Remove any excess glue with a paper towel, and let dry completely, about 4–6 hours, before attaching findings. Let the glue cure for at least 24 hours before wearing.

FIG | 1

FIG | 2

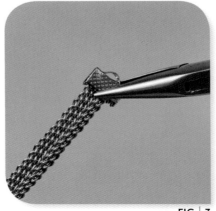

FIG | 3

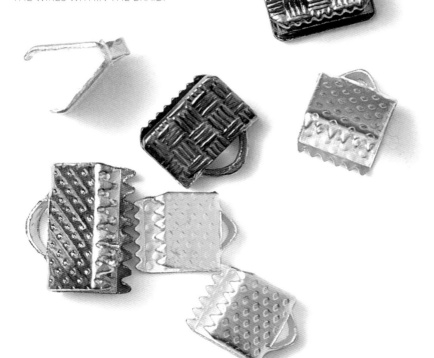

ATTACHING FINDINGS

With a ribbon end secured on your braid, you're ready to attach a finding. The process is the same whether attaching a clasp, extender chain, or earring post. To attach a finding, you will need two pairs of flat-nose or chain-nose pliers (or one of each) and a jump ring.

1 Find the opening in the jump ring, then place one pair of pliers on each side and push the pliers in opposite directions (one away from yourself and one towards yourself). Put the open jump ring through the loop in the ribbon end and attach your finding **(FIGURE 4)**.

2 Close the jump ring in the same manner you opened it, only moving the pliers against each other until they meet. Your finding is now attached **(FIGURE 5)**.

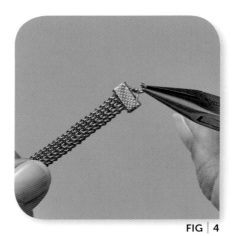

FIG | 4

FIG | 5

LOBSTER CLAW CLASPS

SHAPING A BRACELET

Once the ends of the braid intended to be a bracelet have been finished, it's time to shape it. There are a couple of ways to do this:

• **Use a bracelet mandrel.** Center the braid on one side of the mandrel with the two ends going straight out to either side **(FIGURE 1)**, then use your fingers to bend the ends of the braid around the mandrel until they meet on the underside of the mandrel. Because the wire tends to spring back out a little after being shaped, it's a good idea to use a slightly smaller size on the mandrel than the size you want to end up with. (It's easier to increase the size if needed once we have the shape in place, by gently sliding the bracelet down the mandrel to a larger size.)

• **Use your hands to shape the bracelet.** Place your fingers anywhere on the bracelet and start to gently bend the bracelet into a curve on one side **(FIGURE 2)**, then move to the opposite side. Continue working from side to side, gradually adding more of a curve into the braid until the two ends meet.

FIG | 1

TIP

IF YOU DON'T HAVE A BRACELET MANDREL, YOU CAN USE ANYTHING YOU HAVE HANDY AT HOME, SUCH AS A CUP OR CONTAINER THAT IS CLOSE TO THE SIZE AND SHAPE YOU WANT YOUR FINAL BRACELET TO BE.

FIG | 2

PATINA FINISH

You can use liver of sulfur to add an interesting patina finish to your final pieces of jewelry. Wire kumihimo is ideal for patina as it takes advantage of all the natural texture within the braid and adds a different dimension to the final look. There are different ways to add patina to your pieces, but one of the easiest ways is to use a patina gel. If you have several pieces of jewelry you would like to patina, I recommend doing them in batches, rather than one piece of jewelry at a time. This not only makes the process easier and faster, it also minimizes exposure to the strong smell of the sulfur.

Be sure to clean the jewelry using warm water and dish soap before adding the patina to help it adhere evenly. Using an inexpensive toothbrush is a great way to clean all the

nooks and crannies of the braid. Follow the manufacturer's instructions for the patina you are using, and make sure to use plastic gloves and work in a well-ventilated area. (Patina is not harmful to work with, but the smell is unpleasant.)

Once you have patinated your piece, create a mix of baking soda and a few drops of water to make a thick paste in a bowl. Then apply the paste with your finger to clean off the patina finish from the high points of the kumihimo, and rinse and dry. Use a polishing cloth to polish the braid and highlight the contrast between the now darkened recesses and the polished high points of the braid.

NOTE | PLAN AHEAD, AND CHOSE THE WIRE FOR YOUR PROJECTS CAREFULLY. IF YOU WOULD LIKE TO PATINA A PIECE OF JEWELRY, MAKE SURE TO USE A COMPATIBLE WIRE THAT ACCEPTS A PATINA FINISH, SUCH AS BARE COPPER OR STERLING SILVER. INEXPENSIVE CRAFT WIRE AND ANTI-TARNISH WIRE WILL NOT WORK FOR PIECES YOU WANT TO PATINA BECAUSE THESE WIRES HAVE A COATING THAT RESISTS OXIDIZATION AND THEREFORE ALSO PATINA. IF YOU WOULD LIKE TO PATINA PIECES OF JEWELRY THAT CONTAIN BEADS WITHIN THE DESIGN, MOST TYPES OF BEADS WILL NOT BE DAMAGED BY THE TREATMENT, BUT AVOID USING POROUS GEMSTONE BEADS, SUCH AS TURQUOISE OR PEARLS.

POLISHING PADS

LIVER OF SULFUR

THE PROJECTS

Now that you are more familiar with the basic braids and techniques, you can create lovely pieces of jewelry. Make the projects as shown or add your own flair by using different materials and experimenting with the basic techniques. For instance, changing the color of beads or using a different color wire than suggested in the project instructions can give a very different look to the final piece, even when using the same techniques. The projects range in difficulty level, so you can choose to start light and ease yourself into it, or jump straight in with the first thing that catches your eye. So get your wire and your kumihimo disk ready, and let's get started.

WIRE
KUMIHIMO

The projects in this section are primarily made with wire, and the basic braids are used in different ways to achieve a variety of results. Some designs use a length of braid as the feature itself, while for others the braid is shaped during or after the braiding to achieve a unique look. You can also change many of the designs by simply adding beads to them. Some projects even show alternatives for the featured design.

ELEGANT

BRACELET

This design can be made with any color wire. Here, I combined silver and copper wire because I love the look and think it makes for very elegant jewelry. I also added twisted wire, which helps emphasize the braid structure. To make this bracelet, work with each group of wires in this design as if they were one length, keeping the wires in each group flat next to each other throughout the braid to achieve an even result.

FINISHED SIZE | 7/16" × 8" (11 mm × 20.5 cm)   **LEVEL** | Beginner

MATERIALS

18⅔' (5.7 m) of silver 22-gauge wire

21' (6.4 m) of copper 26-gauge wire
OR
9⅓' (2.8 m) of copper 22-gauge pre-twisted wire

2 ribbon ends (13 mm)

3 jump rings (5 mm)

1 lobster claw clasp

Extender chain

TOOLS

Measuring tape

Wire cutters or flush cutters

Electrical tape

Square kumihimo disk

2 pairs of flat-nose and chain-nose pliers

E6000 glue

1 Cut the 22-gauge wire into fourteen 16" (40.5 cm) lengths.

2 Cut the 26-gauge wire into seven 36" (91.5 cm) lengths. Fold one wire in half and twist it together (see Twisted Wire in Basic Techniques), so you end up with one 16" (40.5 cm) length of twisted wire. Repeat this step for all seven wires.

3 Place three wires lying next to each other in this order: one silver wire, one twisted wire, and one regular wire. Make sure the twisted length of wire is in the middle. Place the rest of the wires in the same pattern, until you end up with seven groups of wire, lying next to each other. Tape all the ends together.

NOTE | EACH GROUP OF 3 WIRES (2 SILVER AND 1 TWISTED) WILL BE TREATED AS IF THEY ARE 1 WIRE.

4 Insert the taped end through the hole in the disk, holding it tightly just underneath. Distribute the groups of wires into the slots according to the Diagonal Kumihimo structure (see Braid Structures). Since there are seven instead of eight groups of wire, you will have four wire groups in top slots 5-8 and three wire groups in bottom slots 5-7 (FIGURE 1).

5 Move the wire group from top slot 5 to right slot B, making sure the wires within that group stay lying flat next to each other as you move them across the disk (FIGURE 2). (To make working with groups of wires easier, see the FIGURE 3 tip.)

6 Move the group of wires from bottom slot 5 into top slot 5, running your fingers as you move them across the middle to make sure they lay flat next to each other (FIGURE 4).

Move the group of wires from top slot 6 to bottom slot 5 (FIGURE 5). Continue working your way toward the right side of the disk, and move bottom slot 6 to top slot 6, top slot 7 to bottom slot 6, bottom slot 7 to top slot 7, top slot 8 to bottom slot 7 (FIGURE 6).

7 Move the group of wires from right slot B into top slot 8, making sure the wires within the group stay lying flat next to each other (FIGURE 7).

8 Repeat steps 5–7 until the lengths of wires are used up. Remove the completed braid and all the wires from the disk. Finish the wires using the ribbon ends, then attach the clasp and extender chain using jump rings.

9 Shape the bracelet to fit (see Shaping a Bracelet in Finishing Kumihimo).

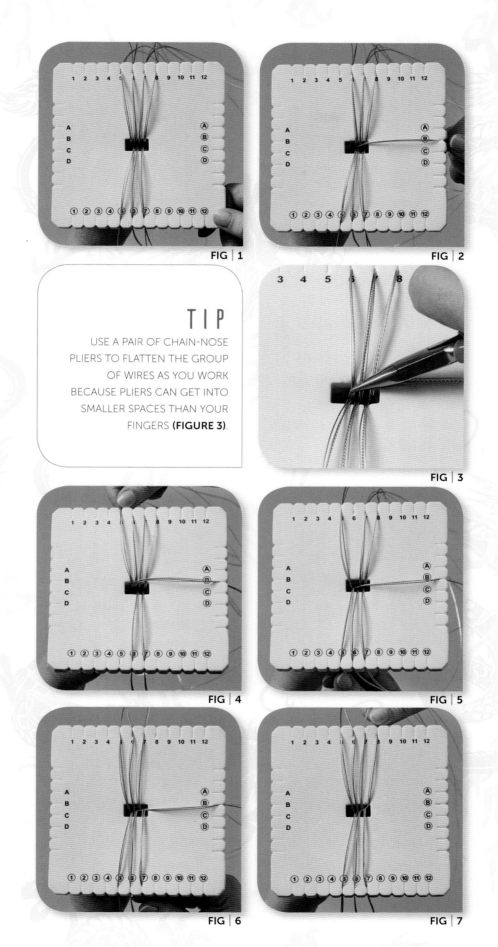

FIG | 1

FIG | 2

TIP

USE A PAIR OF CHAIN-NOSE PLIERS TO FLATTEN THE GROUP OF WIRES AS YOU WORK BECAUSE PLIERS CAN GET INTO SMALLER SPACES THAN YOUR FINGERS **(FIGURE 3)**.

FIG | 3

FIG | 4

FIG | 5

FIG | 6

FIG | 7

INFINITY

RING

When I was coming up with designs for this book, I knew I wanted to make a wire kumihimo ring. I also knew it would be challenging. A ring isn't the most obvious piece of jewelry when making wire kumihimo as the design needs to be delicate, and you also have to find a way to deal with the ends of the braid. I thought of this design one night while falling asleep that incorporated the ends of the wires back into the braid to finish them off and make a continuous ring. The design itself is pretty simple and can be made to fit any size ring.

FINISHED SIZE | ½" (1.3 cm) wide   **LEVEL** | Intermediate

MATERIALS
6⅔' (2 m) of 22-gauge wire

TOOLS
Measuring tape

Wire cutters and flush cutters

Electrical tape

Square kumihimo disk

Ring mandrel

A pair of chain-nose pliers

The Infinity Ring with a patina finish.

1 Cut eight 10" (25.5 cm) lengths of 22-gauge wire. Arrange the wires so they lie flat next to each other and tape them together about 2" (5 cm) from one end.

2 Put the taped end through the center of the disk, holding it tightly just underneath. Distribute the long ends of the wire on the disk according to the Diagonal Kumihimo structure (see Braid Structures), so you end up with four wires in the top middle slots and four wires in the middle slots on the bottom **(FIGURE 1)**. Make a 3" (7.5 cm) long diagonal braid for a size 7 ring.

NOTE | THERE IS ⅛" (3 MM) DIFFERENCE IN BRAID LENGTH BETWEEN HALF SIZES. FOR EXAMPLE, A SIZE 6½ RING REQUIRES A 2⅞" (7.3 CM) LONG BRAID. A SIZE 7½ RING REQUIRES A 3⅛" (8 CM) LONG BRAID, WHICH REQUIRES THE WIRE TO BE ⅛" (3 MM) LONGER OR SHORTER THAN A SIZE 7 RING. USE THIS SIZING TECHNIQUE FOR ANY RING SIZE.

3 Remove the braid from the disk. Bring the wire that was going out to the side in the final round of making the braid back out to the side, so it's facing away from the other wires. There should be four wires pointing towards the back of the braid, three wires pointing towards the front of the braid, and the one wire pointing out to the right side. Push the three wires that are pointing towards the front down against the braid, so they wrap around the wire that is going straight out to the right side. Wrap the wire furthest to the right that is pointing towards the back of the braid around the wire pointing out toward the right in the opposite direction **(FIGURE 2)**.

4 Using flush cutters, cut all three bent wires below where they wrap around the wire pointing out to the side **(FIGURE 3)**.

5 Using a pair of chain-nose pliers, tuck the cut ends of the wires down so they nestle back in toward the braid **(FIGURE 4)**.

6 Repeat steps 3-5 on the opposite end of the kumihimo braid.

7 Wrap the braid around the ring mandrel according to size, making sure the unfinished wires on each end are pointing straight out on the ends away from the braid **(FIGURE 5)**. Remove the braid from the mandrel. Using a pair of chain-nose pliers and working on one end at a time, curve the end of the braid towards the main area of the ring band **(FIGURE 6)**. When both ends are facing toward the braid, thread the wires through the corresponding four loops on the edges of the braid that are directly across from the end of the braid, and pull the wires tight. Repeat this step on the other end **(FIGURE 7)**. Make sure the end of the braid is tight against the edge by pulling on one length of wire at a time with your chain-nose pliers.

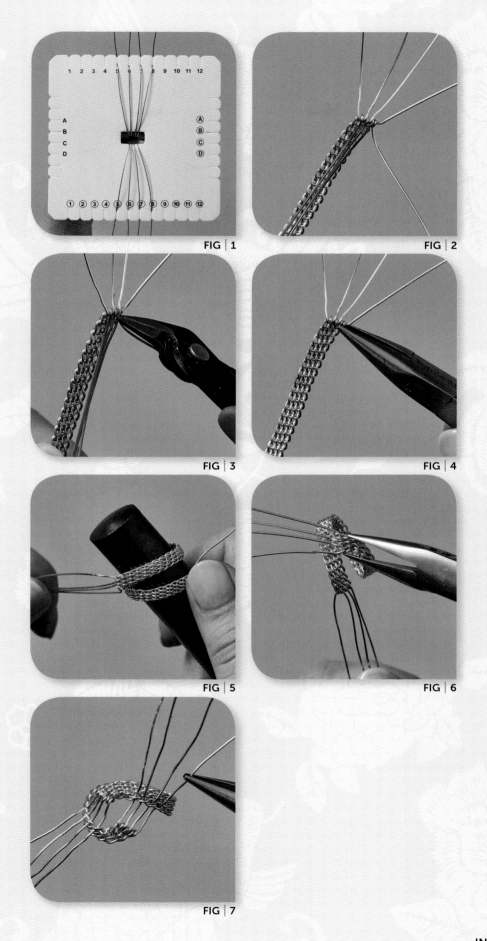

FIG | 1

FIG | 2

FIG | 3

FIG | 4

FIG | 5

FIG | 6

FIG | 7

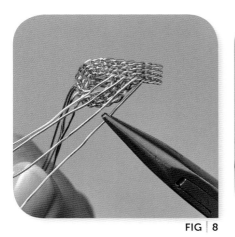

FIG | 8

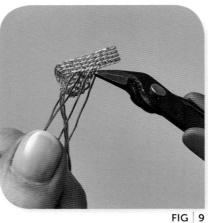

FIG | 9

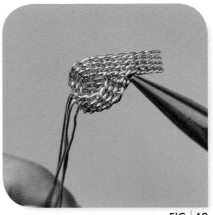

FIG | 10

8 To finish the ends, bend them back around the edge, following the ridge between the loops, so the wire blends into the edge of the braid **(FIGURE 8)**. Using flush cutters, trim the excess wire close to the connection point between the end and edge of the braid **(FIGURE 9)**. Using chain-nose pliers, tuck the ends into the edge of the braid **(FIGURE 10)**. Repeat this step on the other end of the braid.

T I P

IT'S EASIER TO GET A GRIP ON THE BRAID AND PERFORM MORE PRECISE BENDING BY USING A PAIR OF CHAIN-NOSE PLIERS INSTEAD OF YOUR FINGERS.

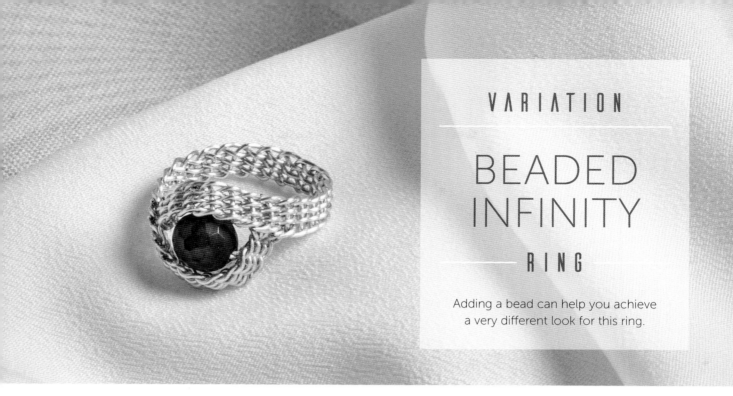

BEADED INFINITY
RING

Adding a bead can help you achieve
a very different look for this ring.

FIG | 11

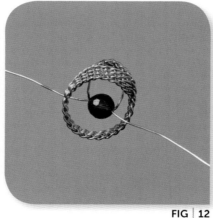

FIG | 12

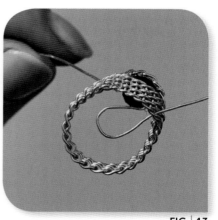

FIG | 13

Adding a bead can help you achieve
a very different look for this ring.

You'll need an 8 mm bead and eight
13" (33 cm) long wires. The braid
starts 4" (10 cm) in from one end
of the wires. For a size 7 ring, use
a 3½" (9 cm) long braid and an
8 mm round bead. When the braid is
complete, finish the ends as in step
3, but don't cut the middle of the
three wires. Shape the braid around
the ring mandrel as in step 7, raising

the braid ends up on their sides to
create a place for the bead. Place
the bead in the middle to use as
a guide and shape the wires around
it if needed **(FIGURE 11)**. Secure the
four ends to the edge of the braid
and finish them as in step 8, leaving
the unfinished wire on each end
out of the way, as you need them
to attach the bead. When the ends
are trimmed and secured, put
both remaining wires through the

bead in opposite directions, then
pull the wires tight so the bead sits
in the center between the ends of
the braid **(FIGURE 12)**. Working with
one wire at a time, put the wires
through a loop on the bottom edge
of the braid opposite the hole in the
bead where the wire is coming out
(FIGURE 13), and finish in the same
way as the other wires.

REGAL

BRACELET

This bracelet uses the Cross Kumihimo structure (see Braid Structures), but it gets a completely different look when using multiple lengths of wire in place of one. The braid itself becomes more substantial, and you can have fun combining different colors in the individual lengths of wire. I used copper with a silver wire accent throughout because it gives a regal look to the final piece and emphasizes the braid structure.

FINISHED SIZE | 1⅜" × 7¾" (3.5 cm × 19.5 cm)   **LEVEL** | Beginner

MATERIALS	TOOLS
16' (4.9 m) of copper 22-gauge wire	Measuring tape
8' (2.4 m) of silver 22-gauge wire	Wire cutters or flush cutters
2 ribbon ends (13 mm)	Electrical tape
3 jump rings (5 mm)	Square kumihimo disk
1 lobster claw clasp	2 pairs of flat-nose and chain-nose pliers
Extender chain	E6000 glue

1 Cut twelve 16" (40.5 cm) lengths of copper wire and six 16" (40.5 cm) lengths of silver wire.

2 Place one copper, one silver, and one copper wire flat next to each other. These three wires form one group and will be acting as a single wire throughout the braid. Repeat this with the remaining wires, making sure to lay the groups flat next to each other for a total of six groups. Tape all the ends together as shown **(FIGURE 1)**.

3 Insert the taped end through the hole in the disk, holding it tightly just underneath. Distribute the groups of wire according to the Cross Kumihimo structure (see Braid Structures), only in a reverse order as there are fewer wires being used to create this braid. Working from the center, place the two middle groups of wire in slots 6 and 7 on the top, the adjacent group on each side of these goes in slots 6 and 7 on the bottom, and the two remaining wires in slots 5 and 8 on the top **(FIGURE 2)**.

4 Move the group from top slot 7 to left slot B, making sure the wires remain flat next to each other in the same order **(FIGURE 3)**. To keep the wires in the same order and help prevent them from crossing, hold the group of wires in the center of the disk with one hand and run the fingers of your other hand along the wires you are moving out to the side. It can also be helpful to use a pair of chain-nose pliers to flatten the individual groups after they have been moved out to the side while making the braid **(FIGURE 4)**.

5 Move the group in top slot 6 to right slot B, again making sure the wires within the group stay flat next to each other and in the correct order **(FIGURE 5)**.

6 Move the group in bottom slot 6 to top slot 6, making sure the wires stay flat next to each other **(FIGURE 6)**. Move the group in top slot 5 to bottom slot 6 **(FIGURE 7)**. Then repeat these two moves on the other side of the disk in a mirror image by moving the group in

bottom slot 7 to top slot 7 and the group in top slot 8 to bottom slot 7 **(FIGURE 8)**.

7 Bring the group of wires on each side of the disk back into the braid: Move the group in left slot B to top slot 5 and the wires in right slot B to top slot 8 **(FIGURE 9)**. This is one full round of movements.

8 Keep repeating steps 4–7 until the desired length is reached or all the wires have been braided, making sure to leave space to attach the ribbon end.

9 Remove the braid from the disk. Measure the length of the braid needed for the final bracelet, taking into account the added length of the clasp, and cut off the excess. Add ribbon ends, and attach the clasp and extender chain with jump rings before shaping the bracelet so it's ready to wear.

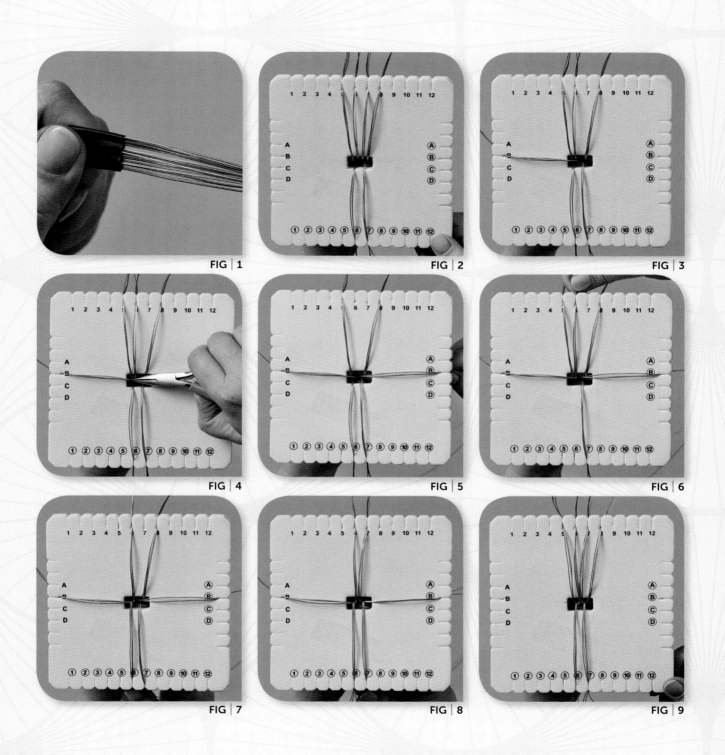

FIG | 1

FIG | 2

FIG | 3

FIG | 4

FIG | 5

FIG | 6

FIG | 7

FIG | 8

FIG | 9

INFINITY

BRACELET

This is one of my first bracelet designs. I thought it would be interesting to combine two different braid structures into one design. The advantage of using wire instead of cord for the braids is the wires stay in place, so they can easily be taken off the disk without worrying about the braid coming undone. As I discovered, experimenting with this technique can lead to many interesting results.

FINISHED SIZE | ½" × 8⅜" (1.3 cm × 21.5 cm)   **LEVEL** | Intermediate

---

MATERIALS	TOOLS
16' (4.9 m) of 22-gauge wire	Measuring tape
2 ribbon ends (8 mm)	Wire cutters or flush cutters
3 jump rings (5 mm)	Electrical tape
1 lobster claw clasp	Square kumihimo disk
Extender chain	2 pairs of flat-nose and chain-nose pliers
	E6000 glue

The Infinity Bracelet looks beautiful with patina aged copper (left) or natural bright silver (right) finish.

1 Cut twelve 16" (40.5 cm) lengths of 22-gauge wire. Lay the wires flat next to each other, lining up the ends. Tape them together near one end.

2 Insert the taped end into the hole in the disk, holding it tightly just underneath. Place the six wires in the middle of the group in slots 4–9 on the top of the disk and the remaining six lengths in slots 4–9 on the bottom **(FIGURE 1)**.

3 Following the Cross Kumihimo structure instructions (see Braid Structures), make a 3¼" (8.5 cm) long braid.

NOTE | TO ACCOMMODATE THE ADDITIONAL FOUR WIRES IN THIS BRAID, WHEN WORKING FROM THE CENTER TO THE LEFT SIDE OF THE DISK, YOU WILL ADD THE ADDITIONAL MOVES: TOP SLOT 4 TO BOTTOM SLOT 5 AND BOTTOM SLOT 4 TO TOP SLOT 4 AT THE END. WHEN CHANGING DIRECTION AND WORKING FROM THE CENTER TO THE RIGHT SIDE OF THE DISK, THE LAST TWO MOVES WILL BE TOP SLOT 9 TO BOTTOM SLOT 8 AND BOTTOM SLOT 9 TO TOP SLOT 9. TO BIND THE BRAID CONTINUE AS DIRECTED, BUT PLACE LEFT SLOT B TO BOTTOM SLOT 4 AND RIGHT SLOT B TO BOTTOM SLOT 9.

4 Switch to the Diagonal Kumihimo structure instructions (see Braid Structures) to make the two braids that will overlap in the center of the design. These braids will naturally form simultaneously side by side, by just altering how you position the two top wires that are placed in the B slots. In the Cross Kumihimo structure, the top wires in slots 6 and 7 cross over each other when placed in the B slots. Here, you won't cross these two wires. Move the wire in top slot 6 to left slot B **(FIGURE 2)** and the wire in top slot 7 to right side B **(FIGURE 3)**. Move the wires on the top and bottom of the disk across to the opposite numbered side in the same way

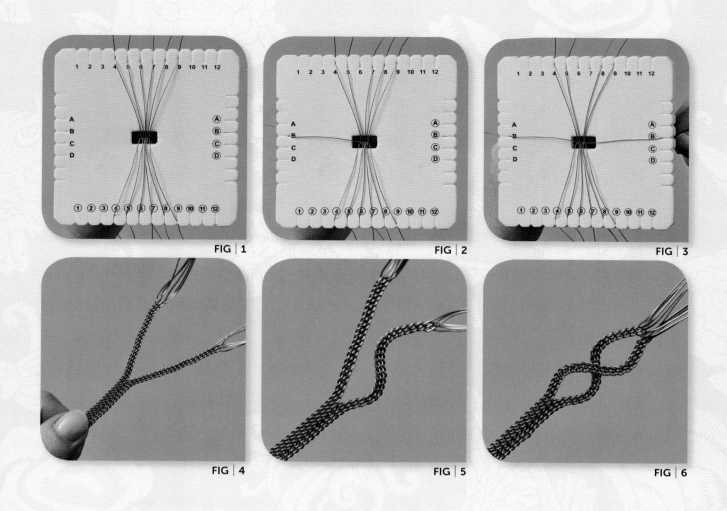

FIG | 1

FIG | 2

FIG | 3

FIG | 4

FIG | 5

FIG | 6

as the Cross Kumihimo structure. Continue creating the two braids next to each other until they are each 1¾" (4.5 cm) long. Remove the braid from the disk and lay the braids horizontally next to each other **(FIGURE 4)**.

5 Shape one diagonal braid into an S shape, with the end finishing on the same level as the beginning **(FIGURE 5)**. Shape the other braid in the same manner in a mirror image while crossing it over the first one, so the two ends are now laying next to each other but have swapped sides **(FIGURE 6)**.

6 Reattach the loose wires back onto the kumihimo disk in the original position for the Cross Kumihimo structure, and hold the ends of the individual braids in place right next to each other with your hand. Restart the Cross Kumihimo by bringing the wire from top slot 7 to left slot B and the wire from top slot 6 to right slot B. Continue this cross-braid structure until you have a 3¼" (8.5 cm) long braid following the middle diagonal kumihimo section.

7 Remove the wire from the disk and finish off the ends using ribbon ends. Attach your clasp, and shape the bracelet into the final shape.

CELTIC INFINITY

This alternative Celtic-inspired design is achieved by shaping the middle part of the bracelet.

FIG | 1

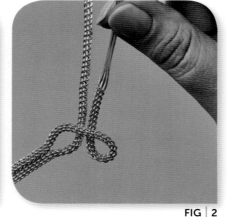

FIG | 2

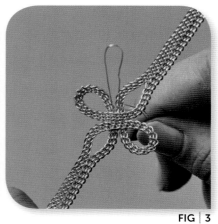

FIG | 3

1 Cut twelve 19" (48.5 cm) lengths of 22-gauge wire and follow steps 2–4 in the Infinity Bracelet directions, making the individual braids in the middle of the bracelet 3" (7.5 cm) long to accommodate the different shape.

2 Remove the wires from the disk. Create the Celtic shape by crossing one braid over the other, while putting a curve into the braids (FIGURE 1). Add a loop to the braid that is crossing over the other braid by bringing it under the top of itself and making sure the loop sits right after the crossover point (FIGURE 2). Add a loop to the other braid by bringing it back underneath itself, and add a curve to both braids when bringing them back into the middle next to each other.

3 Repeat step 6 in the Infinity Bracelet instructions to finish the braid.

4 Cut 8" (20.5 cm) of 26-gauge wire. Leaving a 1" (2.5 cm) tail, thread the wire through the gaps in the braids where they overlap each other in the middle, to connect and fasten the large loops together (FIGURE 3). After the loops are secure, finish the wires by cutting the excess and tucking both ends.

SUNRISE

EARRINGS

The inspiration for these earrings came from Peruvian threading, which uses a thin thread to achieve a pattern within a shape. I thought it would be perfect to use wire kumihimo to create the external shape, then use the gaps in the braid to achieve the threading effect using a thinner gauge wire. The final result offers a lovely vision of the sun rising on the horizon, but using different colors of wire could also create fun and interesting looks.

FINISHED SIZE | 1¼" x 1¾" (3.2 cm x 4.5 cm)   **LEVEL** | Beginner

MATERIALS

16' (4.9 m) of silver 22-gauge wire

24" (61 cm) of copper 22-gauge wire

5⅝' (1.8 m) of copper 26-gauge wire

2 ribbon ends (10 mm)

2 jump rings (5 mm)

2 earring findings

TOOLS

Measuring tape

Wire cutters or flush cutters

Electrical tape

Square kumihimo disk

2 pairs of flat-nose and chain-nose pliers

E6000 glue

1 Cut eight 12" (30.5 cm) lengths of 22-gauge silver wire. Tape the wires together at one end. Insert the taped end through the hole in the disk and hold it tightly underneath, then distribute the wires on the kumihimo disk according to the Diagonal Braid structure instructions in Braid Structures **(FIGURE 1)**. Make one 5½" (14 cm) long braid, and remove it from the disk.

2 Shape the braid into a teardrop shape by bending the two ends toward each other with one side overlapping the other **(FIGURE 2)**.

NOTE | THE FRONT OF THE PIECE IS THE FLATTER SIDE OF THE BRAID.

3 Cut one 12" (30.5 cm) length of 22-gauge copper wire. Attach the wire from the underside to one end of the braid through a loop on the outer edge, leaving a 1" (2.5 cm) tail. Thread the long end of the wire, going from the underside, through the next loop so that the wire overlaps the edge **(FIGURE 3)**. Pull the wire tight so it nestles into the space between the silver wires. Put your wire through the next loop in the same manner, and continue this step around to the other end.

4 Cut one 35" (89 cm) length of 26-gauge copper wire. Securely attach the wire through a loop on the inside edge of the braid, about ¼" (6 mm) below where the braids overlap, leaving a 1" (2.5 cm) tail. Wrap the wire around the same edge wire twice to secure it, and have the long end exiting out the front side **(FIGURE 4)**.

5 Begin the center threading. Bring the wire across the front and down through a wire edge just to the right of the middle of the inner curve, so it is exiting out the backside **(FIGURE 5)**. Bring the wire across the back and through the wire edge just below the wrapped wire in step 4, so the wire is exiting out the front **(FIGURE 6)**. Then bring the wire across the front, and put it through the wire edge just to the right where the wire passed through previously **(FIGURE 7)**. Repeat this pattern to build up the inner embellishment until you have wrapped the inner edge, and the wire is exiting through the wire edge on the opposite of where the initial wire started. Wrap the wire edge twice to securely attach this end of the wire **(FIGURE 8)**.

6 To finish the ends of the copper wire, trim the excess wire with flush cutters close to the edge of the braid. Then use chain-nose pliers to tuck the ends against the braid.

7 Cut the ends of the braid to achieve a straight line **(FIGURE 9)**. If desired, cut away the inner corners of the ends to make them as flat as possible, so they fit inside the ribbon end **(FIGURE 10)**. Fasten the ribbon end with glue, and use a jump ring to attach your earring finding.

8 Repeat steps 1–7 to make the second earring.

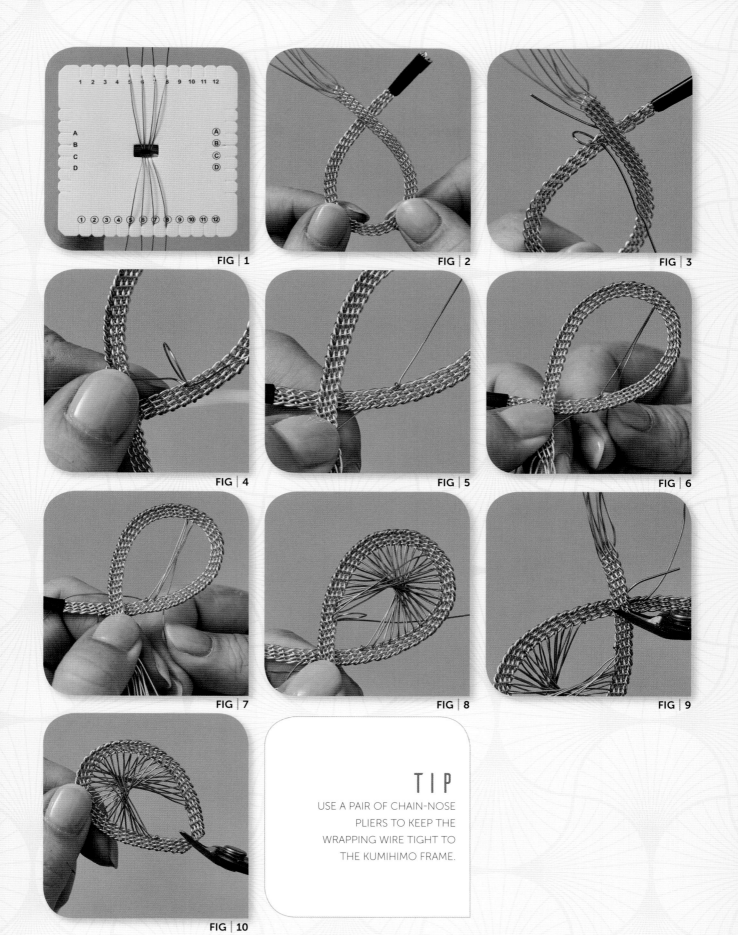

FIG | 1

FIG | 2

FIG | 3

FIG | 4

FIG | 5

FIG | 6

FIG | 7

FIG | 8

FIG | 9

FIG | 10

TIP

USE A PAIR OF CHAIN-NOSE
PLIERS TO KEEP THE
WRAPPING WIRE TIGHT TO
THE KUMIHIMO FRAME.

KYS

BRACELET

Kys means *kisses* in Danish and since Xs are the universal symbol for kisses, I thought that would be an appropriate name for this design, while also referencing my roots. My heart will always be in Denmark, and this piece helps symbolize that for me. It uses a basic wire kumihimo that is embellished by adding two separate lengths of wire after the braid is completed.

FINISHED SIZE | ¼" × 8⁵⁄₁₆" (6 mm × 21 cm)   **LEVEL** | Intermediate

---

MATERIALS	TOOLS
14' (4.3 m) of silver 22-gauge wire	Measuring tape
32" (81 cm) of copper 22-gauge wire	Wire cutters or flush cutters
2 ribbon ends (8 mm)	Electrical tape
3 jump rings (5 mm)	Square kumihimo disk
1 lobster claw clasp	2 pairs of flat-nose and chain-nose pliers
Extender chain	E6000 glue

The flatter side of the braid is considered the front.

1 Cut twelve 14" (35.5 cm) lengths of 22-gauge silver wire. Tape the wires together at one end.

2 Insert the taped end through the hole in the disk and hold it tightly underneath. Distribute the wires following the Cross Kumihimo structure instructions in Braid Structures **(FIGURE 1)**. Braid the wires until you have used the entire length. Remove the braid from the disk.

NOTE | TO ACCOMMODATE THE ADDITIONAL FOUR WIRES IN THIS BRAID, WHEN WORKING FROM THE CENTER TO THE LEFT SIDE OF THE DISK, YOU WILL ADD THE ADDITIONAL MOVES: TOP SLOT 4 TO BOTTOM SLOT 5 AND BOTTOM SLOT 4 TO TOP SLOT 4 AT THE END. WHEN CHANGING DIRECTION AND WORKING FROM THE CENTER TO THE RIGHT SIDE OF THE DISK, THE LAST TWO MOVES WILL BE TOP SLOT 9 TO BOTTOM SLOT 8 AND BOTTOM SLOT 9 TO TOP SLOT 9. TO BIND THE BRAID CONTINUE AS DIRECTED, BUT PLACE LEFT SLOT B TO BOTTOM SLOT 4 AND RIGHT SLOT B TO BOTTOM SLOT 9.

3 Cut two 16" (40.5 cm) lengths of 22-gauge copper wire. Thread one end of a copper wire through a loop on the edge of the finished braid near one unfinished end, leaving a 1" (2.5 cm) tail. Then thread the other copper wire through the corresponding loop on the opposite edge (the loops will vary and not align exactly evenly due to the braid structure), making sure the long ends are coming out toward the front of the braid **(FIGURE 2)**.

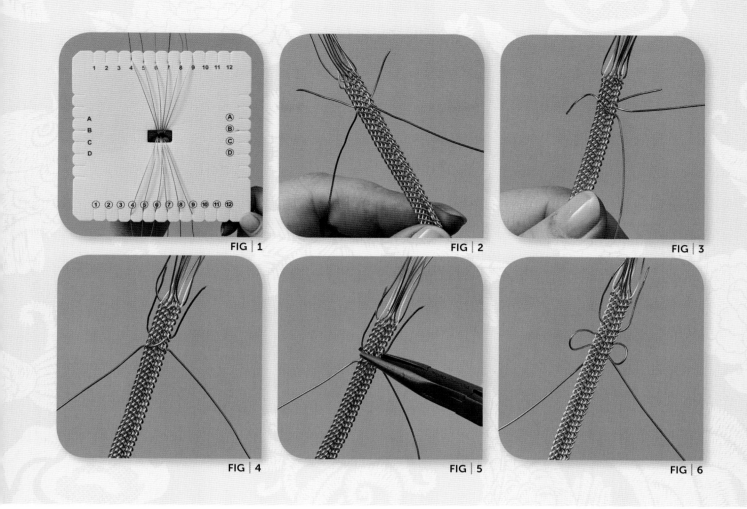

FIG | 1 FIG | 2 FIG | 3
FIG | 4 FIG | 5 FIG | 6

4 Working away from this end of the braid, take the wire that is positioned slightly below the opposite wire, and cross it diagonally to the other edge. Skip a loop, and thread the wire front to back through the following loop on the same edge, so there is an empty loop between them **(FIGURE 3)**. Working in the same manner, bring the second top wire diagonally through a loop on the opposite edge, again skipping one loop and going through the second, so the wire crosses over the other one **(FIGURE 4)**. These movements create the X pattern. Using a pair of flat-nose pliers, gently flatten the X down on the braid **(FIGURE 5)**.

5 Flip the braid over to the back, where the wires are now exiting. Working with one wire at a time, skip the next adjacent edge loop and thread the wire from bottom to top through the following loop. This will place the wire back exiting the front of the braid **(FIGURE 6)**. Repeat this step with the other wire. Pull the wires tight to make them lie along the edge of the braid on either side. Use a pair of flat-nose pliers to push the wires down so they are tight to the braid.

6 Flip the braid back to the front, and repeat steps 4–5 until you have reached the other end of the braid with the Xs. Make sure the copper wires used to make the Xs are finalized on the back of the braid as they will be cut down and go inside the ribbon end along with the braid. For reference, my bracelet contains nineteen Xs.

7 Finish the braid with ribbon ends, use jump rings to attach a clasp and extender chain to each end, and shape the bracelet for wearing (see Shaping a Bracelet in Finishing Kumihimo).

INFINITY

NECKLACE

This is the necklace variation of my Infinity Kumihimo designs. It is a simple design with big impact that can be worn with the Infinity Bracelet and Ring for a complete set. I used a simple chain to not distract from the piece, but you can choose a different chain or even make your own. To make a more delicate version of this design, use a finer gauge wire and a shorter braid length. Regardless of how you choose to make your braid, finishing the piece with patina adds a lovely depth that really makes the braid and the shape stand out.

FINISHED SIZE | 1" x 2⅜" (2.5 cm x 6 cm)   **LEVEL** | Intermediate

MATERIALS	TOOLS
8⅔' (2.7 m) of 20-gauge wire	Measuring tape
5 jump rings (4 mm)	Wire cutters and flush cutters
Chain	Electrical tape
1 lobster claw clasp	Square kumihimo disk
Extender chain	2 pairs of chain-nose and flat-nose pliers
	Fine round-nose pliers

1 Cut eight 13" (33 cm) lengths of 20-gauge wire. Place the wires evenly and tape them together about 2" (5 cm) from one end.

2 Insert the taped end through the hole in the disk and hold it tightly just underneath. Distribute the wire on the disk according to the Diagonal Kumihimo structure in Braid Structures **(FIGURE 1)**. Create a 5⅜" (13.5 cm) braid and remove it from the disk.

3 Prepare one end of the braid to connect to the center of the braid. Bring the wire that was going out to the side in the final round of making the braid back out to the side, so the wire is facing away from the other wires. There should be four wires pointing upward towards the back of the braid, three wires pointing towards the front of the braid, and the one wire pointing out to the right side. Press the three lengths down flat against the front of the braid, so they continue to wrap on top of the wire that is going out to the side. Bend the wire furthest to the right of the four that are pointing up and away from the braid down against the back of the braid, so it also wraps around the wire going out to the side in the opposite direction of the previous wires **(FIGURE 2)**.

4 Trim the excess wire of each of the four bent wires just below the point where they wrap on top of the side wire **(FIGURE 3)**. Using chain-nose pliers, press each wire end so it nestles back into the braid **(FIGURE 4)**. Repeat on both ends, so there are four lengths of wire left on each end.

5 Start shaping the braid into the infinity symbol by bending the ends in a loop back toward the middle in opposite directions, making sure the middle of the braid stays straight **(FIGURE 5)**.

> **NOTE** | EACH END OF THE BRAID WILL MEET UP WITH ITS OWN SIDE OF THE STRAIGHT MIDDLE SECTION. BRING THE LONG ENDS OF THE WIRE FROM ONE END UNDER THE MIDDLE, AND THE WIRES FROM THE OTHER END OVER THE MIDDLE TO MAKE SPACE FOR THEM AS SHOWN.

6 Working with one side at a time, widen the infinity loop slightly, so there is space to work. Insert the four wire ends through the four loops on the side of the middle section of the braid where the end of the braid meets it **(FIGURE 6)**. Pull each length of wire using your chain-nose pliers until the end is tight against the side **(FIGURE 7)**. Repeat with the other end of the braid, so both ends are attached to the middle.

7 Bring each wire in the direction of the braid, so they follow the ridge between the loops created by the braid structure on the side. Working on one side at a time, bring the two outer wires through the loop around to the back of the braid, making sure to follow the ridge **(FIGURE 8)**.

8 Turn the braid over. Using flush cutters, trim the excess wire where it was bent around the edge **(FIGURE 9)**. With a pair of chain-nose pliers, press the end of the wire so it nestles back into the braid.

9 Turn the braid front-side up and cut off the excess of the remaining two wires and nestle the ends down into the braid as before. Repeat on the other side to complete the infinity symbol **(FIGURE 10)**.

10 On the front of the piece, choose one top loop on the outer edge on each side that are even with each other. Working from the front, widen one loop with a pair of fine round-nose pliers **(FIGURE 11)**. Insert a jump ring, then attach one end of the chain **(FIGURE 12)**. Repeat on the other side. Attach a clasp and extender chain on each end of the chain so the Infinity Necklace is ready to wear.

FIG | 1   FIG | 2   FIG | 3

FIG | 4   FIG | 5   FIG | 6

FIG | 7   FIG | 8   FIG | 9

FIG | 10   FIG | 11   FIG | 12

CELTIC

EARRINGS

I wanted to make a pair of wire kumihimo earrings in a different style. I decided to use a basic braid, then shape it into a Celtic-inspired knot. Using a wire braid worked well because it holds the shape. The earrings look lovely in wire, but you can also add beads for extra interest and movement. Whether you use beads or not, finishing with patina adds an enchanting antique look that complements the Celtic style (see Patina Finish in Finishing Kumihimo for details).

FINISHED SIZE | 1⅜" × 2¼" (3.5 cm × 5.5 cm)   **LEVEL** | Intermediate

MATERIALS	TOOLS
16' (4.9 m) of 22-gauge wire	Measuring tape
16" (40.5 cm) of 26-gauge wire	Wire cutters and flush cutters
2 ribbon ends (8 mm)	Electrical tape
2 jump rings (5 mm)	Square kumihimo disk
2 earring findings	2 pairs of chain-nose and flat-nose pliers
	E6000 glue

1 Cut six 16" (40.5 cm) lengths of 22-gauge wire. Tape the wires together near one end.

2 Insert the taped end through the hole in the disk and hold it tightly just underneath. Distribute the wires on the disk according to the Diagonal Kumihimo structure (see Braid Structures) so there is a length of wire in slots 5–7 on the top and bottom of the disk.

3 Move the wire from top slot 5 to right slot B, then move the wire from bottom slot 5 to top slot 5. Bring the wire from top slot 6 to bottom slot 5. Continue working the diagonal braid structure: Move bottom 6 to top 6, top 7 to bottom 6, and bottom 7 to top 7. Move the wire from right side B to bottom slot 7, so the wires are back in the original position. Continue braiding using the diagonal kumihimo technique until you have incorporated all of the wire. Remove the braid from the disk.

4 With the front of the braid facing up, create a ¾" (2 cm) curve at one end of the braid, then put a small curve into the very end of the braid in the opposite direction, so you end up with a slight S-shape (FIGURE 1).

5 Make a ¾" (2 cm) loop a bit further down the braid by bringing the long end of the braid back underneath itself (FIGURE 2). Make a slightly larger loop (about ⅞" [2.2 cm]) by bringing the braid back over itself, so the two parts of the braid end up next to each other (FIGURE 3).

6 Bring the braid back underneath itself to make the next ¾" (2 cm) loop on the other side. Complete the first loop to make the second half similar to the first. Using your fingers, shape the final design so it is as symmetrical as possible (FIGURE 4).

7 Cut 8" (20.5 cm) of 26-gauge wire. Put one end through the gaps in the braid, where it is crossing over itself, leaving a 1" (2.5 cm) tail.

Weave the wire through the middle loops on the front of the design to secure them together (FIGURE 5). Weave the wire all the way around the middle, then trim the excess wire with flush cutters (FIGURE 6). Tuck the ends with chain-nose pliers, so they nestle into the braid (FIGURE 7).

8 Cut straight across the two braids at the top to get a flat edge (FIGURE 8). To make sure the ends of the braid don't overlap, cut the inner corners of the ends. Add glue to the inside of your ribbon end and clamp it down over the ends of the braid. Attach the earring findings to the ribbon end using a jump ring.

9 Repeat steps 1–8 to make the second earring. When making the matching earring, it's helpful to use the first one as a guide for the shape, so you can make them as even as possible.

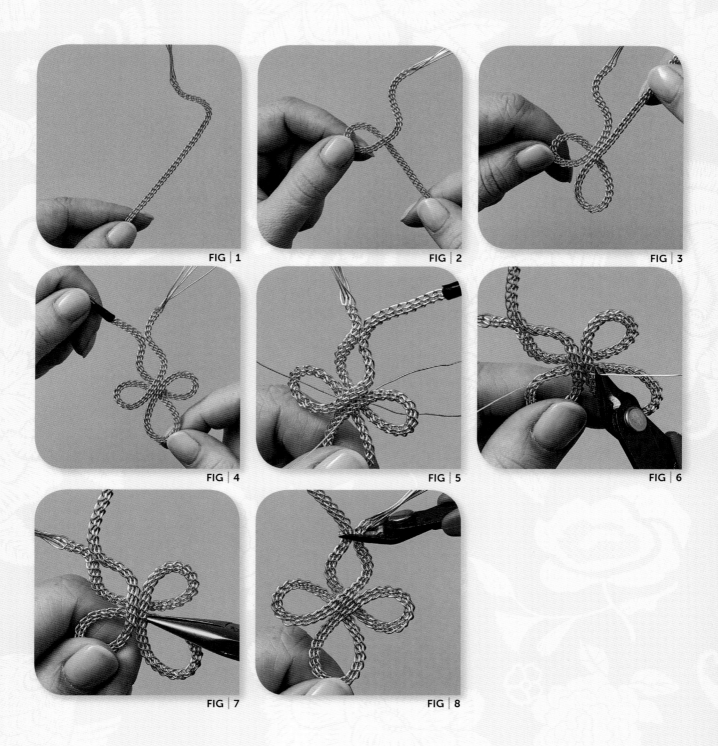

FIG | 1

FIG | 2

FIG | 3

FIG | 4

FIG | 5

FIG | 6

FIG | 7

FIG | 8

FIG | 10

FIG | 11

FIG | 12

FIG | 13

When adding beads to the earrings, choose a loop on the lower edge of each braid loop, making sure the side loops are even with one another. Enlarge the three loops slightly with the tip of a pair of fine round-nose pliers (**FIGURE 10**). Put one bead onto a head pin and make a 90-degree bend above the bead using your chain-nose pliers, then make a loop right after the bend using a pair of round-nose pliers. Slide the loop of the head pin through one of the loops you widened in the braid (**FIGURE 11**). Grab onto the loop with your chain-nose pliers and wrap the end of the head pin around itself above the bead to complete the wire-wrapped loop. Trim the excess head pin wire (**FIGURE 12**), and flatten the end so the bead hangs below the loop as shown (**FIGURE 13**). Repeat this step with the other two loops you have prepared in the braid for each earring.

WATERFALL

EARRINGS

While I was creating the designs for this book, working on one design would often spark the idea for another. These earrings were one of those inspirations. The idea came to me while I was making the Cabochon Necklace. I thought about using the ends of the braid to finish off the piece, but also wanted to make them a feature of the design itself. They give a wonderful waterfall effect, and you can also add beads to emphasize it.

FINISHED SIZE | 1⅜" × 2¼" (3.5 cm × 5.5 cm) **LEVEL** | Intermediate

---

MATERIALS

18⅔' (5.7 m) of 22-gauge wire

2 jump rings (5 mm)

2 earring findings

TOOLS

Measuring tape

Wire cutters or flush cutters

Electrical tape

Square kumihimo disk

2 pairs of chain-nose and flat-nose pliers

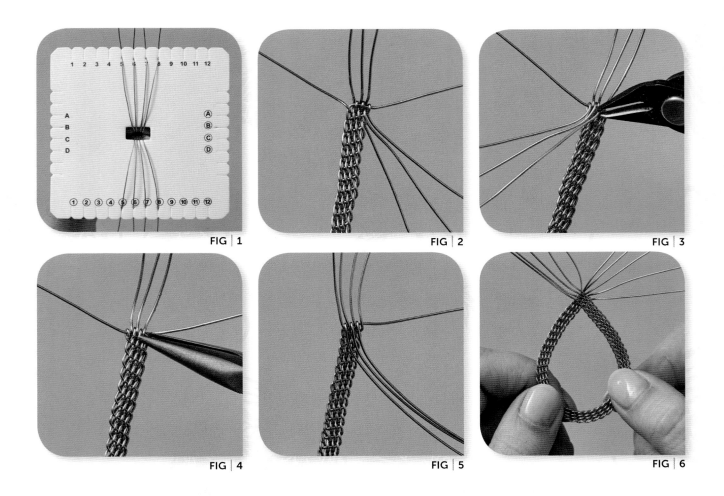

FIG | 1

FIG | 2

FIG | 3

FIG | 4

FIG | 5

FIG | 6

1 Cut eight 14" (35.5 cm) lengths of 22-gauge wire. Tape the wires together about 4" (10 cm) from one end.

2 Insert the taped end through the hole in the disk and hold taped section tightly just underneath. Distribute the wires into the slots on the disk according to the Diagonal Kumihimo structure in Braid Structures, with wires in slots 5–8 on the top of the disk and slots 5–8 on the bottom of the disk **(FIGURE 1)**.

3 Make a 5" (12.5 cm) braid. Remove the wires from the disk and smooth them out with your fingers. On both ends, bring the wire that was going out to the side in the final round of making the braid back out to the side, so it's facing away from the other wires.

4 Hold the braid vertically front-side up with the ends sticking out as shown, so the left end of the braid has four lengths of wire pointing toward the front, three lengths pointing toward the back, and one wire going out to the side. Of the four wires pointing toward the front, push the three wires on the right against the braid **(FIGURE 2)**. Trim the wires just after where they have been bent **(FIGURE 3)**. Using

chain-nose pliers, push the ends down so they nestle back in toward the braid **(FIGURE 4)**.

5 On the other end of the braid there will be three wires pointing towards the front, four wires pointing towards the back and one wire straight out to the side. Push the three front wires against the braid **(FIGURE 5)**. Cut off the excess wire in the same manner as the other end. Again, push the ends in towards the braid using your chain-nose pliers.

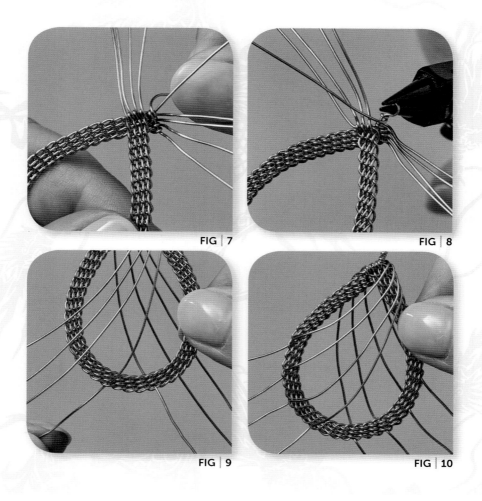

FIG | 7

FIG | 8

FIG | 9

FIG | 10

6 Place the braid in a horizontal position on your work surface, with the ends pointing out to the sides. Working from the middle out to the sides, curve the ends of the braid toward each other. Overlap the ends slightly to create a teardrop shape **(FIGURE 6)**. Wrap one of the two middle wires around the base of the other middle wire twice to attach them together **(FIGURE 7)**. Trim the excess of the wrapped wire and tuck the end with chain-nose pliers. Make a 90-degree bend in the remaining middle wire slightly above the wraps, then make a wire-wrapped loop using round-nose pliers, wrapping the wire around itself until it meets the previous wraps **(FIGURE 8)**. Trim and tuck the end.

7 Hold the braid with the front facing you and four lengths of wire going out to each side. Bring the top right wire across the front of the braid toward the left side, leaving a curve in the wire while moving it. Bring the next wire down in the same direction, leaving some space between the wires. Continue with the remaining wires until you have brought all four down to the opposite side. Turn the piece over and repeat with the remaining four wires on the opposite side.

8 Turn the piece to the front. Locate the middle loop on the bottom outer edge of the curved braid directly opposite the point at the top. Skip one loop going out toward the left, and put the bottom length of wire on the top right side through the next loop from top to bottom. Pull the length through, keeping the curve sweeping across the piece **(FIGURE 9)**. Grasp the adjacent wire on the top right side, skip two loops to the left of the wire just threaded, and bring this wire through the third loop on the left side of the braid. Repeat this last move with the remaining two top wires on the right side. Flip the earring over to the backside, and repeat this entire step to add embellishment wires on this side of the earring **(FIGURE 10)**.

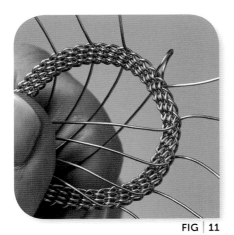

FIG | 11

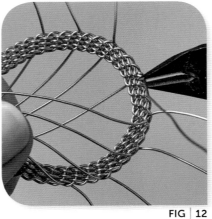

FIG | 12

FIG | 13

9 Working with one wire at a time, thread the wire through the loop right next to it from top to bottom, and pull it tight. Make sure to follow the direction of the braid so the wire nestles into the ridge on the edge when pulled tight **(FIGURE 11)**.

> **TIP**
> TO GET A BETTER GRIP, USE A PAIR OF CHAIN-NOSE PLIERS TO INSERT THE WIRE THROUGH THE LOOP AND PULL IT TIGHT.

10 When all eight wires have been brought through the adjacent loop in the previous step, bring each wire around the braid's edge, and trim the excess wire, leaving a very short length on the other side **(FIGURE 12)**. Push the end of the wire against the braid using chain-nose pliers, so it nestles back in towards the braid **(FIGURE 13)**. Repeat with the remaining wires. Attach the earring finding to the wire wrapped loop on the top using a jump ring.

11 Repeat steps 1–10 to make the second earring but in a mirrored image, so the wires sweep across in the opposite direction to create a complementary pair.

To make beaded earrings, add beads to the wires in step 8 before inserting the ends of the wires through the loops on the bottom of the teardrop shape **(FIGURE 14)**. Once the beads have been added, finish the earrings according to the directions. (I used 2 mm round beads in my design.)

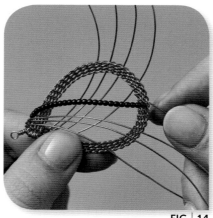

FIG | 14

ETERNAL LOOPS

NECKLACE

I wanted to make a wire kumihimo necklace with the braid as the focus in a more traditional pendant style. I also wanted to use the braid to make an attractive shape that would sit nicely on the neckline. To achieve this, I made a longer basic braid and shaped it afterwards. Using different colors of wire can completely change the look, and the necklace can be finished off using either chain or stringing material.

FINISHED SIZE | 3" × 3" (7.5 cm × 7.5 cm)   **LEVEL** | Beginner

MATERIALS	TOOLS
19⅓' (5.9 m) of 22-gauge wire	Measuring tape
3⅓' (1 m) of 26-gauge wire	Wire cutters or flush cutters
2 ribbon ends (6 mm)	Electrical tape
5 jump rings (5 mm)	Square kumihimo disk
1 lobster claw clasp	2 pairs of chain-nose and flat-nose pliers
Extender chain	E6000 glue

1 Cut eight 29" (73.5 cm) lengths of 22-gauge wire. Tape the wires together toward one end. Insert the end through the hole in the disk and hold it tightly just underneath. Distribute the wires on the disk according to the Diagonal Kumihimo structure with wires in slots 5–8 on the top and bottom of the disk. Make a 20" (51 cm) braid, then remove the wires from the disk.

2 Lay the long braid horizontally on a surface front-side up. Find the middle of the braid, then bring the two ends closer to each other until they overlap and create a 1¼" (3.2 cm) teardrop shape from tip to bottom, making sure the braid stays flat while shaping it **(FIGURE 1)**.

3 Start adding a curve into the right side of the braid just after where the braid overlaps, then bring the braid back over itself to form a 1¼" (3.2 cm) teardrop shape from tip to bottom that is at a slight angle. Make a matching loop on the opposite side **(FIGURE 2)**.

T I P

WHILE MAKING THE LOOPS, KEEP THE PIECE FLAT BY PRESSING DOWN ON THE BRAID NEAR THE OVERLAPPING POINTS **(FIGURE 3)**.

4 Make a smaller final loop on the right side measuring about 1" (2.5 cm) from tip to bottom with the end of the braid going straight up. Make the final loop on the left side the mirror image of the loop just made **(FIGURE 4)**.

5 To make the shape more stable, cut an 8" (20.5 cm) length of 26-gauge wire. Where the braid overlaps in five spots, insert the end of the wire through both layers in the gaps within the braid, leaving a 1" (2.5 cm) tail. Go back and forth through the braid several times, pulling the wire tight and securing it in place **(FIGURE 5)**. Cut the excess wire leaving a short end **(FIGURE 6)**. Using chain-nose pliers, tuck the short end into the braid.

6 Cut the end of the braid just after the final loop on both sides, leaving a short length (about ¼" [6 mm]) that fits inside the ribbon ends **(FIGURE 7)**. Attach the ribbon ends on each side using glue and flat-nose pliers, making sure the ends sit evenly, so the piece will hang straight when adding the chain. Using jump rings, attach the chain to the ribbon ends, and then add the clasp and extender chain to the chain.

T I P

WORKING WITH THESE LONG LENGTHS OF WIRE FOR THE BRAID CAN BE DAUNTING, SO TAKE YOUR TIME AND SMOOTH OUT THE LENGTHS EACH TIME YOU MOVE THEM ON THE DISK TO KEEP THEM FROM TANGLING.

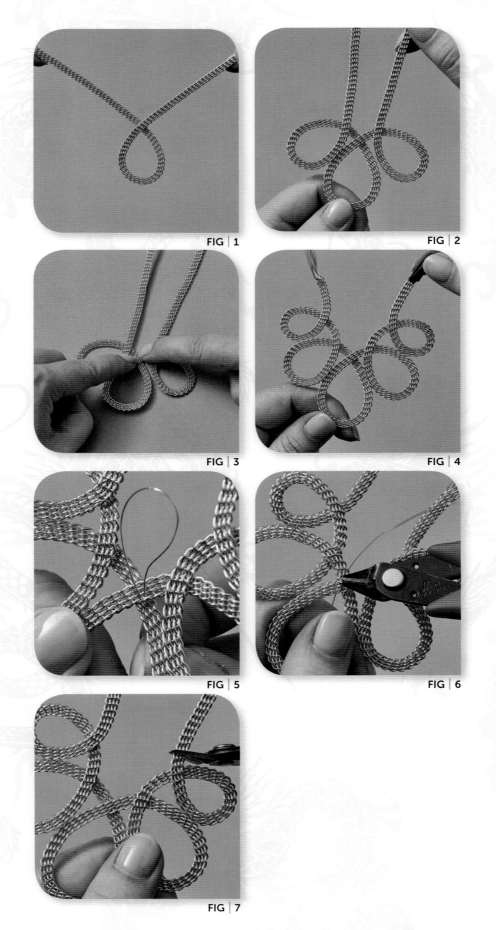

FIG | 1

FIG | 2

FIG | 3

FIG | 4

FIG | 5

FIG | 6

FIG | 7

BEADED ETERNAL LOOPS

For a different look, add beads to your necklace.

FIG | 1

FIG | 2

FIG | 3

1 Once the shape is completed and the overlapping points are secure, cut 17" (43 cm) of 22-gauge wire. Thread one end through a loop on the outer edge of the braid from underneath, starting from the narrow tip of the small teardrop shape on the right side, leaving a 1" (2.5 cm) tail. Next thread the long end of the wire from underneath through the following adjacent loop below it **(FIGURE 1)**. Pull the wire tight. Continue weaving the wire through the next loop until you reach the lower part of this teardrop **(FIGURE 2)**. Follow the structure of the braid, so the wire tucks into the ridge between the loops on the edge.

2 Add one 2 mm, one 3 mm, and one 2 mm bead to the wire to bridge the gap to the next teardrop shape, then insert the wire through the corresponding loop on the outer edge of the upper side of the next teardrop shape **(FIGURE 3)**.

3 Weave the wire as before through each loop on this teardrop shape until you reach the lower part of the wide curve in this teardrop, then add one 2 mm, one 3 mm, one 4 mm, one 3 mm and one 2 mm bead to the wire. Go through the corresponding loop on the outer edge of the large teardrop.

4 Continue around the bottom edge of the large teardrop shape, and add the beads in a mirror image on the left side. Finish the wire in the same location where you started, except ending on the left side of the piece. Trim the excess wires leaving a short tail, then tuck the ends using chain-nose pliers.

TIP
PLAY AROUND WITH THE BEADS TO ACHIEVE DIFFERENT LOOKS.

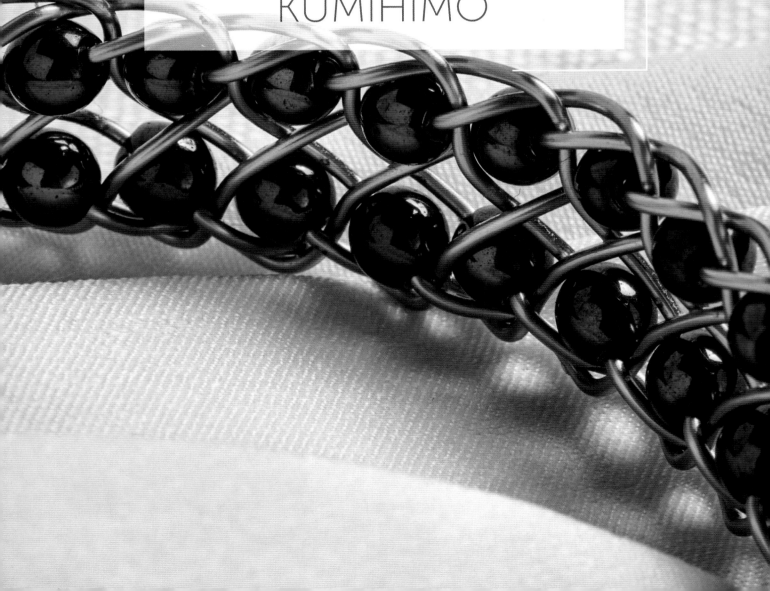

BEADED
WIRE
KUMIHIMO

In this section, you will find wire kumihimo designs incorporating beads. Different kinds of beads are used throughout the projects and within most of them, the beads can be swapped for other beads,depending on what you like. So there is plenty of room for experimentation. The beads are an important part of many of the designs, which simply would not be possible without them as the beads help give a certain shape or look to the braid. Have fun with these projects, and remember to play around with the types of beads you use for your pieces.

CHANDELIER

EARRINGS

The braid for this pair of earrings acts as a skeleton shape on which beads hang to create a chandelier effect. You can use any beads you like, such as bicone crystals for an elegant look or colored beads for a playful finished result. You can also change the size of the earrings by making the initial braid longer if you prefer larger earrings. Either way they are perfect for a special occasion.

FINISHED SIZE | 1¼" x 2⅛" (3.2 cm x 5.5 sm) **LEVEL** | Advanced

MATERIALS

17' (5.2 m) of 20-gauge wire

Approximately 70 bicone crystals (2.5 mm)

Approximately 70 ball-end head pins

2 jump rings (5 mm)

2 earring findings

TOOLS

Measuring tape

Wire cutters or flush cutters

Electrical tape

Square kumihimo disk

2 pairs of chain-nose and flat-nose pliers

1⅛" (3 cm) stepped mandrel

Fine round-nose pliers

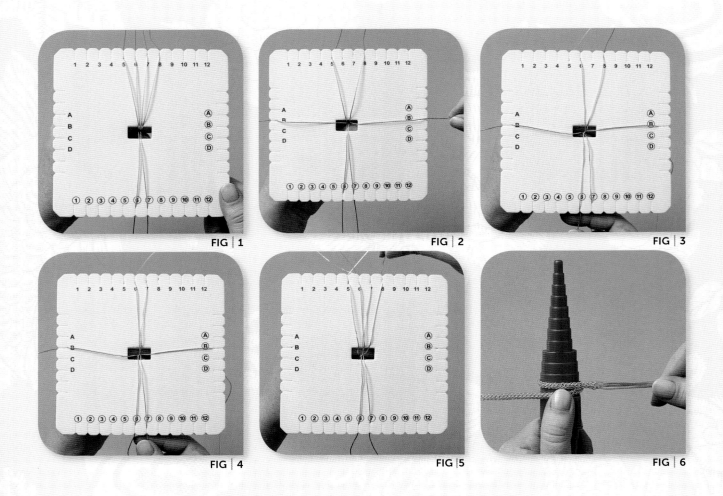

FIG | 1

FIG | 2

FIG | 3

FIG | 4

FIG | 5

FIG | 6

1 Cut six 17" (43 cm) lengths of 20-gauge wire. Tape the wires together about 1½" (3.8 cm) from one end.

2 Insert the taped end through the hole in the disk and hold it tightly underneath. Place the two middle wires in slots 6 and 7 on the top of the disk. Place the wires on either side into slots 6 and 7 on the bottom of the disk and the final two wires into the slots 5 and 8 on the top of the disk (FIGURE 1).

3 Following the Cross Kumihimo structure (see Braid Structures), move the wire from top slot 7 to left slot B and the wire from top slot 6 to right slot B (FIGURE 2). Move the wire in bottom slot 6 to top slot 6 and the wire in top slot 5 to bottom slot 6 (FIGURE 3). Then move the wire in bottom slot 7 to top slot 7 and the wire in top slot 8 to bottom slot 7 (FIGURE 4). Place the wire from left slot B in top slot 5 and the wire in right slot B in top slot 8 (FIGURE 5). The wires are now back in the original position. Continue this technique to create a 9½" (24 cm) long braid.

4 Remove the wires from the disk. Place the braid front-side up on a 1⅛" (3 cm) mandrel, leaving a 1⅛" (3 cm) length going out to the side. Wrap the long end of the braid around the mandrel (FIGURE 6). Continue wrapping the braid around a gradually smaller mandrel until the whole length is used up. Remove the braid from the mandrel (FIGURE 7).

NOTE | CHECK FROM ABOVE OR BELOW TO MAKE SURE THE BRAID IS FORMING AN EVEN SPIRAL (FIGURE 8).

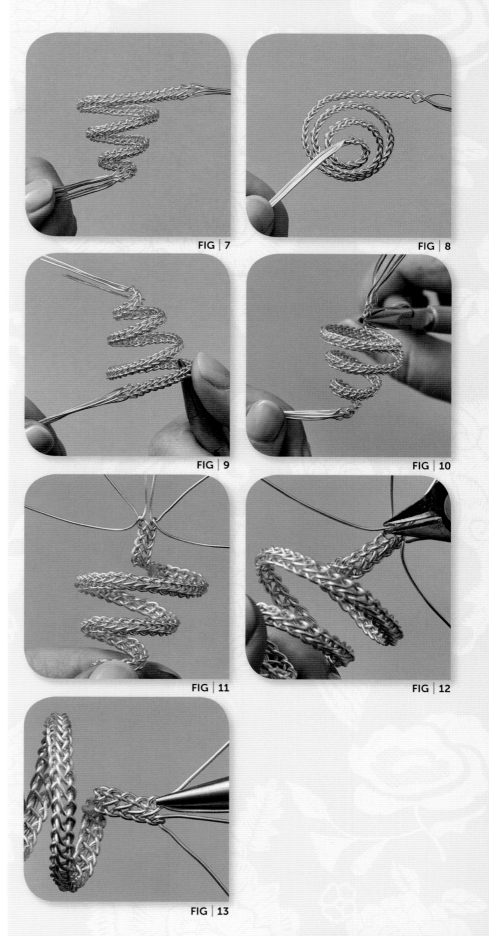

5 Place the tip of chain-nose pliers about 1⅛" (3 cm) from the end of the braid with the largest circle. Push against the pliers with your thumb to make a 90-degree angle **(FIGURE 9)**, so this end is going straight across the middle of the circle. Twist the end away from the braid, then place the chain-nose pliers halfway across the short end just created, and make another 90-degree bend **(FIGURE 10)**. If necessary push this end down slightly, so it is level with the large circle.

6 There are now six wires sticking up from the braid. Wrap each of the wires pointing out to the side around the wire next to it, so the wires are twisting up away from the braid **(FIGURE 11)**. Cut the excess wire on both sides where the wrap ends **(FIGURE 12)**. Then push the ends of the wire down with chain-nose pliers **(FIGURE 13)**.

FIG | 7

FIG | 8

FIG | 9

FIG | 10

FIG | 11

FIG | 12

FIG | 13

7 Cross one of the middle wires over the other, then wrap the crossing wire around the other again **(FIGURE 14)**. Trim the excess wire and push the end down. Wrap the two remaining outer wires around the middle wire **(FIGURE 15)**, then cut the excess wires one at a time.

8 Use the remaining wire to make a wire-wrapped loop. Bend the wire 90 degrees with chain-nose pliers approximately ⅛" (3mm) above where the braid ends, then use round-nose pliers to make a loop **(FIGURE 16)** and wrap the wire below it. Trim the excess wire, and push the wire end down **(FIGURE 17)**. Finish the other end of the braid in the same manner but make an open loop instead of a wrapped loop. Trim the excess wire, and flatten the loop with chain-nose pliers to close it.

9 Add a 2.5 mm bicone crystal to a head pin, then make a 90-degree bend in the head pin just above the bead. Using round-nose pliers, make a loop above the crystal. Attach the loop to the open loop at the bottom loop in the braid. Complete the loop by wire-wrapping the head pin above the crystal, trim the excess wire, and push the end down so it isn't sticking out. Move up two loops on the lower outer edge of the braid, and widen this loop slightly with the tip of fine round-nose pliers **(FIGURE 18)**. Prepare the next head pin with a bead, add it to the loop, and finish it as before **(FIGURE 19)**.

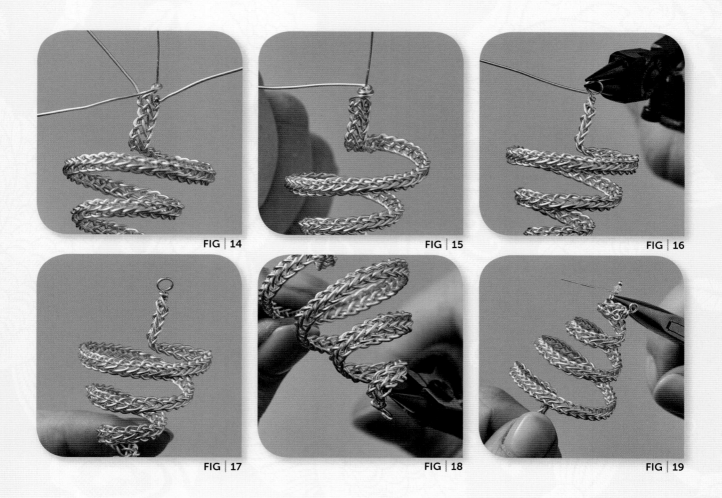

FIG | 14

FIG | 15

FIG | 16

FIG | 17

FIG | 18

FIG | 19

Continue skipping one loop and adding a head pin with a bead to the second loop until you reach the top. For reference, my earrings contain 34–37 crystals each.

NOTE | WHEN MOVING FURTHER UP THE PIECE, IT CAN BE HELPFUL TO MANEUVER THE HEAD PIN BETWEEN THE LOOPS USING CHAIN-NOSE PLIERS TO GET IT INTO A POSITION WHERE YOU CAN MAKE A WRAPPED LOOP.

10 Add an earring finding to the top loop using a jump ring.

11 Repeat steps 1–10 to create the second earring, making it a mirror image of the first to complete the pair. When wrapping the braid around the mandrel, wrap the long end above the short end instead of underneath, then continue making the spiral shape. This will ensure the earrings hang opposite each other when worn with the beginning of the large circle pointing away from your face.

EDGY

BRACELET

When I started experimenting with wire kumihimo, this was the first design with beads I created. It is a basic braid that was completely transformed when beads were added. And it can have many different looks depending on the materials used. It can be on the bolder side by using thicker wire and stronger color beads, or have a more elegant look by using finer wire and more delicate beads such as bicones. Once you have the Cross Kumihimo structure down, this is a great design to try as you can easily achieve a wonderful result with a basic skill level.

FINISHED SIZE | ⅜" × 8⅝" (1 cm × 22.5 cm)   **LEVEL** | Beginner

MATERIALS	TOOLS
9½' (2.9 cm) of 20-gauge wire	Measuring tape
48 rounds (3 mm)	Wire cutters or flush cutters
2 ribbon ends (10 mm)	Electrical tape
3 jump rings (5 mm)	Square kumihimo disk
1 lobster claw clasp	2 pairs of flat-nose and chain-nose pliers
Extender chain	E6000 glue

1 Cut eight 14" (35.5 cm) lengths of 20-gauge wire. Tape the wires together at one end.

2 Insert the taped end through the hole in the disk and hold it tightly underneath. Distribute the wires on the disk following the Cross Kumihimo structure in Braid Structures **(FIGURE 1)**, then braid four full rounds (you will need this length to finish the bracelet).

3 For the fifth round, move the wire in top slot 7 to left slot B and the wire in top slot 6 to right slot B **(FIGURE 2)**. Move the wire in bottom slot 6 to top slot 6 and the wire in top slot 5 down to the bottom slot 6. Release the wire in bottom slot 5 and smooth it out with your fingers, then add one bead **(FIGURE 3)**. Push the bead down to the braid, then move this wire to top slot 5. Make sure the bead tucks underneath the wire crossing out to the side of the disk to hold it in place on the edge of the braid **(FIGURE 4)**.

4 Repeat these steps on the other side of the disk by moving the wire in bottom slot 7 to top slot 7. Continue moving your way toward the right, and move the wire in top 8 to bottom 7. Release the wire in bottom slot 8, smooth it out with your fingers, and then add a bead **(FIGURE 5)**. As you move this length of wire to top slot 8, make sure the bead is tucked underneath the wire going out to the side of the disk to hold it in place **(FIGURE 6)**.

5 Bring the wires on the side of the disk back into the braid by moving the wire in left side B into bottom slot 5 and the wire in right side B into bottom slot 8 **(FIGURE 7)**.

6 Repeat another round of cross kumihimo without adding any beads, then work as before to create an additional round with beads. Continue alternating the braiding pattern in this manner of adding beads every other round.

7 Once all of the beads have been added, finish the braid by making another four rounds without beads.

8 When the braid is complete, remove the wires from the disk, and finish the bracelet using ribbon ends. Attach the clasp and extender chain using jump rings, and shape the bracelet as desired.

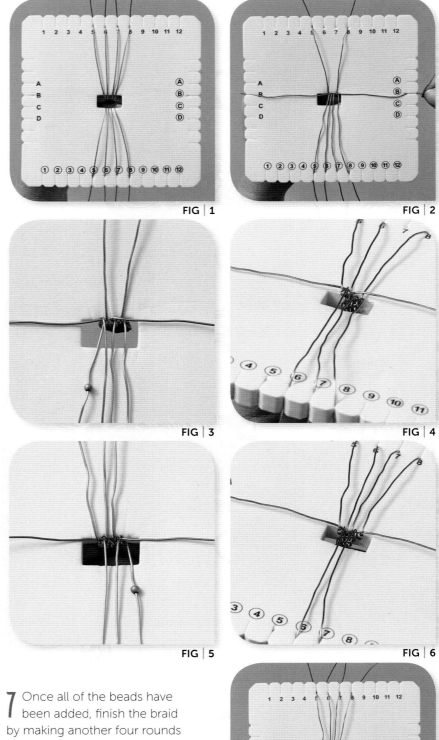

FIG | 1

FIG | 2

FIG | 3

FIG | 4

FIG | 5

FIG | 6

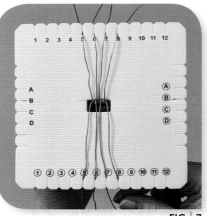

FIG | 7

CRYSTAL EDGY

For an even more elegant design, combine eight 14" (35.5 cm lengths of 22-gauge wire with 2.5 mm Swarovski bicone crystals. To achieve the same length of braid, you'll need to use 58 bicones.

NOTE | ADJUST THE LENGTH OF THE BRACELET BY MAKING THE BRAID SHORTER OR LONGER. SIMPLY MEASURE THE BRAID WHILE YOU ARE MAKING IT TO KNOW WHEN TO FINISH BRAIDING. REMEMBER TO TAKE INTO ACCOUNT THE LENGTH OF THE CLASP WHEN MEASURING THE BRACELET.

TIP
MAKE SURE THE HOLES IN THE BEADS ARE LARGE ENOUGH TO FIT THE WIRE.

COLLAR

NECKLACE

I was inspired to make a beaded kumihimo necklace using the diagonal braid structure, but also wanted to have a curve in the braid so it would lie nicely when worn. I used different size beads to help achieve this effect, then attached chain to each end of the braid to turn it into a necklace with the braid as the center piece.

FINISHED SIZE | ¾" × 3¼" (2 cm × 8.5 cm)   **LEVEL** | Intermediate

MATERIALS

8¼' (2.5 m) of 20-gauge wire

12 rounds (4 mm)

11 rounds (6 mm)

10 rounds (8 mm)

2 ribbon ends (10 mm)

5 jump rings (5 mm)

1 lobster claw clasp

Extender chain

TOOLS

Wire cutters or flush cutters

Electrical tape

Square kumihimo disk

2 pairs of flat-nose and chain-nose pliers

E6000 glue

1 Cut seven 14" (35.5 cm) lengths of 20-gauge wire. Tape the wires together near one end.

2 Insert the taped end through the hole in the disk, and hold it tightly just underneath. Set up the disk according to the Diagonal Kumihimo structure in Braid Structures, making note that only three wires will be placed in the bottom of the disk. In this instance, bottom slot 8 won't contain a wire **(FIGURE 1)**.

3 Because the top of the disk has four wires, move the wire in top slot 5 to right slot B. Move the wire in bottom slot 5 to top slot 5, then move the wire from top slot 6 to bottom slot 5. Continue working in diagonal kumihimo, and move bottom 6 to top 6, top 7 to bottom 6, bottom 7 to top 7, and top 8 to bottom 7. Bring the wire on right side B back into the braid by placing it in top slot 8. The wires are now back in the original position and this is considered one full round of the braid structure. Create 4 more rounds, so you have a section of braid to use for finishing off the piece later.

4 Before starting the next round, release the wire and add a 4 mm round bead to the wire in bottom slot 5, a 6 mm round bead to the wire in bottom slot 6, and an 8 mm round bead to the wire in bottom slot 7 **(FIGURE 2)**. Push the beads all the way down the wires so they are on top of the end of the braid.

TIP
BECAUSE THE WIRE BRAID WITHOUT BEADS IS TIGHTER, MAKE MORE SPACE FOR THE BEADS BY GENTLY PUSHING THE LENGTHS OF WIRE OUT TO THE SIDES TO MAKE SPACE BETWEEN THEM.

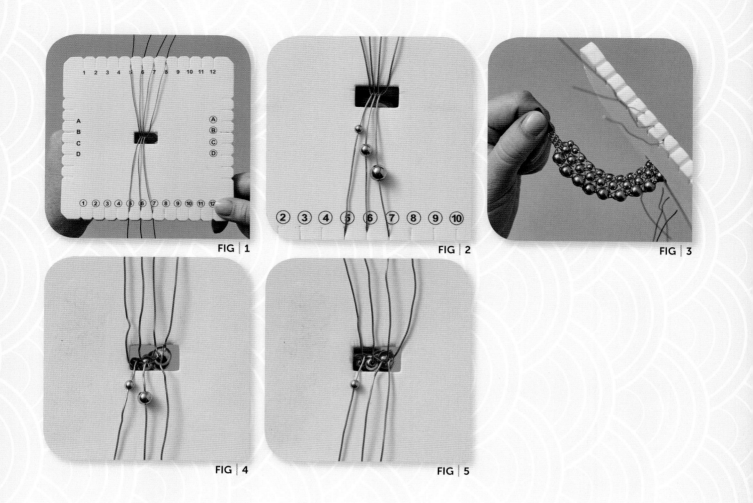

FIG | 1

FIG | 2

FIG | 3

FIG | 4

FIG | 5

5 For the following round work as in step 3, except incorporate the beads just added into the braid. Make note: When moving the wire in top slot 5 to right slot B, make sure the wire is on top of the beads when bringing it over. When repeating the steps of bringing the top and bottom wires to the opposite sides, make sure the beads stay in position while moving the wires. Also, make sure the beads stay underneath the wire in right slot B during each move. For example, when moving the wire in bottom slot 5 to top slot 5, make sure the bead stays under the wire that is crossing out to the side in slot B.

6 Repeat step 5 until there are 10 rows with beads **(FIGURE 3)**. You will notice a natural curve in the beadwork that is achieved by adding the smaller beads on one side, and the larger beads on the other side.

7 To complete the beaded section, make another round of the braid, except add only the 4 mm and 6 mm beads, leaving out the 8 mm bead **(FIGURE 4)**. Then work another round adding only a 4 mm round bead **(FIGURE 5)**. Finish the braid by making four rounds with only the wire, just like the beginning, so you have the same length on each side to finish off the ends.

8 To finish the ends, cut the excess wire and attach the ribbon ends. Add a jump ring to each ribbon end, attach your desired length of chain on both ends, and use a jump ring to attach a lobster claw clasp and extender chain to each end of the chain.

NOTE | THE LENGTH OF THE CHAIN ON EACH SIDE WILL DETERMINE THE FINAL LENGTH OF THE NECKLACE. YOU CAN CHOOSE TO USE EITHER ONE SINGLE LENGTH OF CHAIN THAT IS LONG ENOUGH TO PUT OVER THE HEAD OR USE TWO EQUAL LENGTHS THAT ATTACH WITH A CLASP IN THE BACK.

SNAKY

BRACELET

This design came about when I was experimenting with how to add beads to basic kumihimo. I added the beads within the braid in a more unusual way, while keeping it a somewhat basic technique. The final result reminded me of snakeskin, so I ended up calling it the Snaky Bracelet. A variety of looks can be achieved by using different materials. Whether you prefer a bolder look or a more elegant design, this bracelet offers many possibilities.

FINISHED SIZE | $9/16$" × $8⅜$" (1.5 cm × 21.5 cm)   **LEVEL** | Intermediate

---

MATERIALS	TOOLS
$10⅔$' (3.3 m) of 20-gauge wire	Wire cutters or flush cutters
62 rounds (4 mm)	Electrical tape
2 ribbon ends (10 mm)	Square kumihimo disk
3 jump rings (5 mm)	2 pairs of flat-nose and chain-nose pliers
1 lobster claw clasp	E6000 glue
Extender chain	

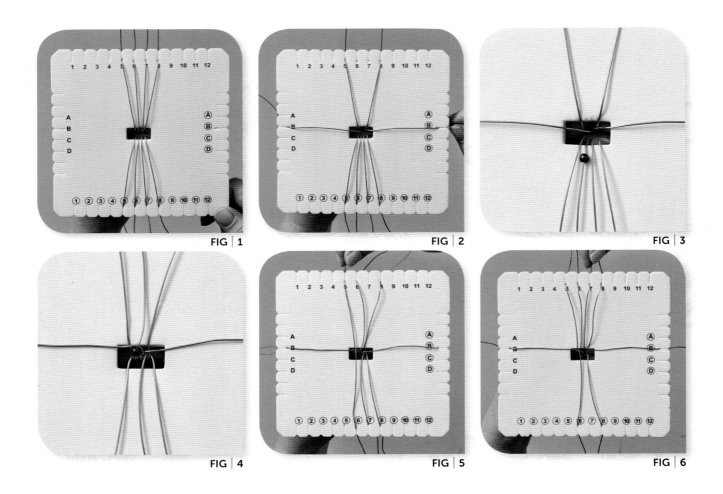

FIG | 1
FIG | 2
FIG | 3
FIG | 4
FIG | 5
FIG | 6

1 Cut eight 16" (40.5 cm) lengths of 20-gauge wire. Tape the wires together near one end.

2 Insert the end of the wire through the hole in the disk and hold it tightly just underneath. Attach the wires to the disk according to the Cross Kumihimo structure in Braid Structures **(FIGURE 1)**.

3 Make four full rounds of the Cross Kumihimo technique on the disk.

4 Start the next round by moving the wire from top slot 7 to left slot B and the wire from top slot 6 to right slot B **(FIGURE 2)**. Release the wire in bottom slot 6 and add a bead **(FIGURE 3)**, pushing it down to the braid so it sits underneath

the wire in left slot B. If needed, lift up the wire in left slot B to make space for the bead. Once you have pushed the bead into place, put the wire with the bead in top slot 6 **(FIGURE 4)**. Move the wire in top slot 5 to bottom slot 6, then move the wire in bottom slot 5 to top slot 5 **(FIGURE 5)**.

5 Repeat these steps on the other side of the disk by adding a bead to the wire in bottom slot 7 and pushing the bead into the gap underneath the wire going out to right slot B before moving it into top slot 7 **(FIGURE 6)**. Move the wire from top slot 8 to bottom slot 7, and bottom slot 8 to top slot 8. Bring the wires on the sides of the disk back into the braid by moving the wire in left

slot B to bottom slot 5 and the wire in right slot B to bottom slot 8. This is one full round of the braid with added beads.

6 Keep repeating steps 4–5 to achieve the full length needed for the bracelet. Measure the braid as you go, taking the clasp into account for the final length. After all of the beads have been added, finish the braid with four rounds of wire-only braiding (no beads). Take the wires off the disk.

7 Finish the braid with ribbon ends. Use a jump ring to attach a lobster claw clasp on one end and an extender chain on the other end. Shape the bracelet for wearing (see Shaping a Bracelet in Finishing Kumihimo).

CRYSTAL SNAKY

An alternative look can be achieved by using different materials with the same techniques. Swapping the 20-gauge wire for 22-gauge, but using the same lengths and using 3 mm Swarovski bicone crystals, for example, can create a completely different and more elegant look.

TEARDROP

EARRINGS

Inspired by the Snaky Bracelet, these are the first wire kumihimo earrings I ever created. I wanted to use the beads in a way that would naturally achieve a curve within the braid to create the teardrop shape. It worked perfectly for a pair of earrings, and if you use similar materials, would make a great set along with the Snaky Bracelet. Being familiar with the Snaky Bracelet would be helpful for creating this design as it is the same basic technique, just slightly more difficult because the curve is being added while making the braid.

FINISHED SIZE | 1¾" × 1⅛" (4.5 cm × 3 cm)   **LEVEL** | Intermediate

---

MATERIALS

13⅓' (4.1 m) of 22-gauge wire

28 rounds (3 mm)

2 ribbon ends (10 mm)

2 jump rings (5 mm)

2 earring findings

TOOLS

Wire cutters or flush cutters

Electrical tape

Square kumihimo disk

2 pairs of flat-nose and chain-nose pliers

E6000 glue

1 Cut eight 10" (25.5 cm) lengths of 22-gauge wire. Tape the wires together near one end.

2 Insert the taped end through the hole in the disk and hold it tightly just underneath. Attach the wires to the disk following the Cross Kumihimo structure instructions in Braid Structures **(FIGURE 1)**. Make a 1" (2.5 cm) braid using just the wire (approximately 7 rounds).

3 Start another round of the braid by moving the wire in top slot 7 to left slot B and the wire in top slot 6 to right slot B. Move the wire in bottom slot 6 to top slot 6. Move the remaining wires on this left half of the disk to the opposite sides by moving the wire in top slot 5 to bottom slot 6 and the wire in bottom slot 5 to top slot 5. Before moving the wires on the right half of the disk, release the wire in bottom slot 7 and add a bead. As you move this wire to the top slot 7, make sure the bead is tucked into the gap underneath the wire crossing out to right slot B **(FIGURE 2)**. If needed, lift up the wire in right slot B to make space for the bead.

4 Move the remaining wires on the top and the bottom sides on this half of the disk to the opposite sides, following the Cross Kumihimo structure of moving top 8 to bottom 7 and bottom 8 to top 8 **(FIGURE 3)**. Bring the wires on the sides of the disk back into the braid one at a time by placing the wire in left slot B in bottom slot 5 and the wire in right slot B in the bottom slot 8.

5 Repeat steps 3–4 until you have added 14 beads into the braid. As you add in the beads, the braid will gradually curve more and more underneath the disk. At one point, the start of the braid will hit the back of the disk **(FIGURE 4)**. To continue braiding, move the braid out of the way by moving the end of the braid to the side as you would open a jump ring from front to back **(FIGURE 5)**, which will gradually create space to continue adding beads into the braid.

6 Make another inch of braid using just the wire to replicate the beginning.

7 Remove the braid from the disk and flatten it out to create the flat teardrop shape. Finish the ends of the braid by cutting off the excess wire with a pair of flush cutters to get a flat edge **(FIGURE 6)**. Attach the ribbon ends using glue and flat-nose pliers **(FIGURE 7)**, then attach the earring finding using a jump ring.

8 Repeat steps 1–7 to make the second earring.

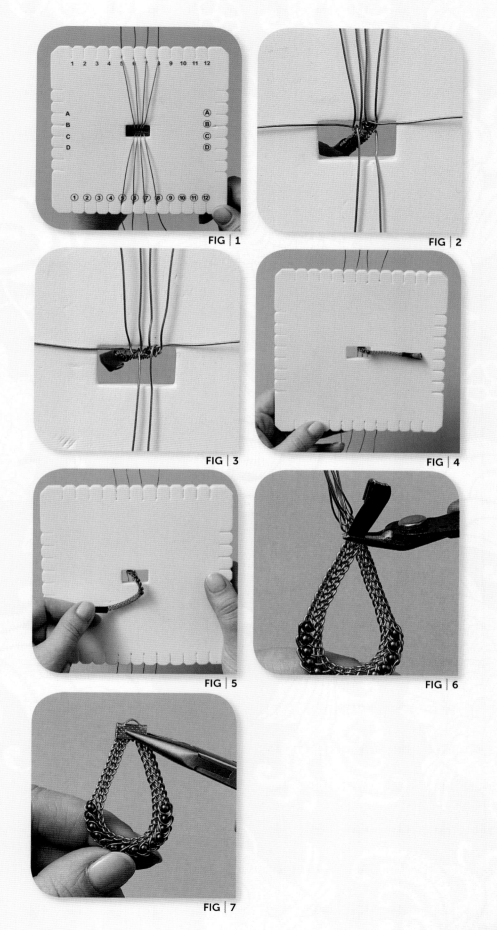

FIG | 1

FIG | 2

FIG | 3

FIG | 4

FIG | 5

FIG | 6

FIG | 7

CABOCHON

NECKLACE

When I was coming up with wire kumihimo designs, I knew I wanted to capture a cabochon with the technique. I developed an idea in my head for how to make it work, and when I made the first test piece it turned out exactly as I imagined. Wire kumihimo is the only technique used throughout the design, and the ends of the braid secure the cabochon.

FINISHED SIZE | 1¼" × 2⅜" (3.2 cm × 6 cm)   **LEVEL** | Advanced

MATERIALS

13⅓' (4.1 m) of 22-gauge wire

One 3 cm × 4 cm teardrop cabochon about 6 mm deep

Chain

2 jump rings (5 mm)

1 lobster claw clasp

Extender chain

TOOLS

Wire cutters or flush cutters

Square kumihimo disk

Approximately ⅛" (3 mm) mandrel

2 pairs of flat-nose and chain-nose pliers

1 Cut eight 20" (51 cm) lengths of 22-gauge wire. Tape the wires together about 8" (20.5 cm) from one end.

2 Insert the taped end into the center of the disk and hold the ends by the tape tightly just underneath. Arrange the wires on the disk following the directions for Cross Kumihimo structure in Braid Structures **(FIGURE 1)**. Braid 4.5" (11.5 cm), and remove it from the disk.

> **NOTE** | THE EXTRA 8" [20.5 CM] OF WIRE WILL BE USED TO MAKE THE BAIL AND CAPTURE THE CABOCHON IN PLACE LATER.

3 Remove the wires from the disk and straighten out the ends of wire that were positioned under the disk (they will be used for the bail and capturing the cabochon) along with the other wires on the opposite end.

4 Place the cabochon on a firm surface facing up. Place the middle of the braid against the bottom of the cabochon with the back of the braid facing the cabochon. The back of the braid is the slightly more rounded side and the front of the braid is the flatter side. Push the braid up each side of the cabochon until the two ends of the braid meet at the top point of the teardrop shape **(FIGURE 2)**. This will help you achieve the right shape easily.

5 Remove the cabochon, and intertwine the lengths of wire at the top by bringing one wire from one end of the braid toward the opposite side, then bring one wire from the other end towards the opposite side. Continue alternating the wires until they have all been combined **(FIGURE 3)**.

6 Place the cabochon face up within the braid, holding it in place to make sure it keeps its size and shape. Bring the wire furthest to the front around the side toward the back, making sure it goes underneath the other wires going out to that side. Bring the next wire in the front that is going toward the opposite side around the side toward the back, underneath

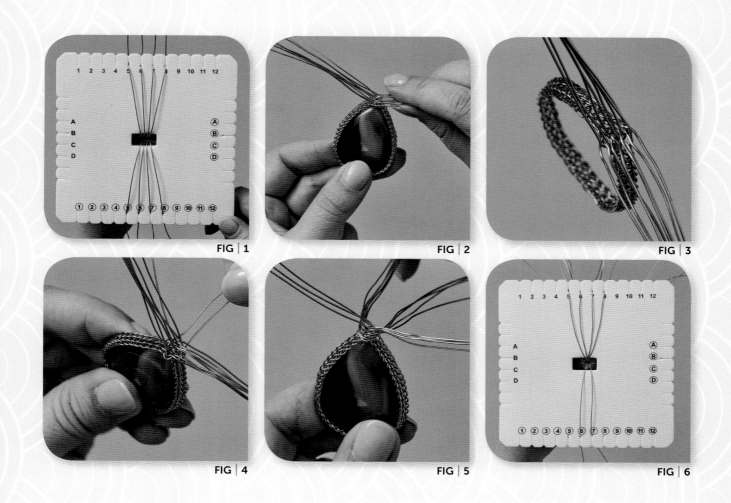

FIG | 1

FIG | 2

FIG | 3

FIG | 4

FIG | 5

FIG | 6

the wires going out to that side **(FIGURE 4)**. Continue working from side to side and moving the next wire further toward the back until you have moved five lengths of wire on each side and have six lengths of wire coming out from the middle **(FIGURE 5)**. These are the wires for making the bail. Remove the cabochon from the braid for now.

7 Move the two front and two back wires for the bail toward the sides they are coming from so they don't cross in the middle. The two middle wires should be crossing over each other toward the opposite side.

8 Reattach the braid to the kumihimo disk by putting the six lengths of wire for the bail through the hole from the bottom, so the braid for the cabochon is directly under the opening. When attaching the wires for the bail to the disk, make sure the ends of the wires below the disk on the back of the cabochon are facing away from you and the front of the piece is towards you. Distribute the wires onto the disk by placing the two front wires in top slots 6 and 7. Place the next two wires to bottom slots 6 and 7, then move the final two wires to top slots 5 and 8 **(FIGURE 6)**.

TIP

THIS TECHNIQUE CAN BE USED FOR MANY DIFFERENT SIZES AND SHAPES OF CABOCHONS JUST BY ADJUSTING THE BRAID LENGTH THAT WRAPS AROUND THE CABOCHON'S EDGE. AN EASY WAY TO DETERMINE HOW LONG TO MAKE THE INITIAL BRAID IS TO TAKE A PIECE OF SCRAP WIRE OR CORD AND MEASURE THE CIRCUMFERENCE OF THE CABOCHON. THAT WILL BE THE BRAID LENGTH NEEDED TO REACH ALL THE WAY AROUND THE CABOCHON.

9 While braiding the bail, hold the shaped braid under the disk, moving your fingers up the braid as it gets longer **(FIGURE 7)**. Continue braiding using the Cross Kumihimo structure as before: Move the wire in top slot 7 to left slot B, then move the wire in top slot 6 to right slot B. Move the wire in bottom slot 6 to top slot 6, then move the wire in top slot 5 to bottom slot 6. Repeat these steps in a mirror image on the other side of the disk: Bottom slot 7 to top slot 8 and top slot 8 to bottom slot 7. Bring the wires on the sides of the disk back into the braid, by moving the wire from left slot B into top slot 5 and the wire from right slot B into top slot 8. The wires are now back in the original position, completing one full round of this braid. Keep repeating the movements in this step for approximately eight rounds until you have a 1" (2.5 cm) braid.

10 Remove the braid from the disk. Gently bend the beginning of the braid forward to make space for the bail. Place a small mandrel behind the middle of the braid, bending the braid around it toward the back until it reaches the beginning of the braid **(FIGURE 8)**. At the open end of the braid, there will be three wires that are naturally going toward the left of the pendant and three wires going toward the right. Keep the wires to their respective sides (they will be used to fasten the bail in place).

11 On the edge of the braid that will be surrounding the backside of the cabochon, there are little loops along the edge. Working on one side at a time, thread the outer wire through the uppermost loop on the same side. Then thread the next wire through the next loop down, and do the same with the third wire on that side. Repeat with the wires on the other side. Pull the wires tight through the loops to bring the end of the bail close to the beginning of the bail **(FIGURE 9)**.

12 Secure the wires in place by wrapping them around the edge toward the back again. Make sure to follow the direction of the braid, so the wire nestles into the well between the loops on the edge of the braid **(FIGURE 10)**. Cut off the excess wire, leaving a little end sticking out towards the back **(FIGURE 11)**. Using chain-nose pliers, push the ends of the wires down against the braid to secure the wires and make sure they aren't sticking out).

> # TIP
>
> **ALTERNATIVE FOR CAPTURING THE CABOCHON**
>
> IF YOU'RE WORRIED YOUR CABOCHON WILL FALL OUT THE FRONT OF YOUR PENDANT, USE A COUPLE OF THE WIRES IN STEP 13 ON THE FRONT OF THE PENDANT. WIRES CROSSING ON THE FRONT AND BACK WILL LOCK THE CABOCHON IN PLACE.

13 Place the cabochon in the braid face-up. Turn the bezel setting over to the back side, and find the midpoint on the bottom of the braid. Bring the bottom wire on the right across the back of the cabochon, then thread it through the third loop to the left of the midpoint. Bring the corresponding bottom wire from the left side down across the cabochon and thread it through the third loop after the midpoint on the right side. The wires should be crossing over each other **(FIGURE 12)**. Go back to the right side, and bring the adjacent wire to the opposite left side. Skip one loop, and thread it through the second loop after the first one. Continue moving from side to side, attaching one wire at a time, always skipping one loop before feeding it through the next one, until you have attached all the loose wires from the top along the edge. Bend all the lengths of wire around the edge back toward the back side of the cabochon. Trim the excess wire, and tuck the lengths one at a time in the same manner as step 12.

14 The cabochon is now captured within the wire kumihimo, and you can use the bail to hang it on a necklace chain.

FIG | 7

FIG | 8

FIG | 9

FIG | 10

FIG | 11

FIG | 12

The back of the
Cabochon Necklace.

STARLIGHT

EARRINGS

This pair of earrings is full of beautiful sparkles. Because a fine wire is used for this braid, it is easy to form into the final teardrop shape without compromising the structure of the braid. I used ribbon ends to finish the ends because they would be difficult to finish otherwise, and we can then easily attach earring findings to them.

FINISHED SIZE | 1½" × 2¼" (3.8 cm × 5.5 cm)   **LEVEL** | Beginner

MATERIALS	TOOLS
32' (9.8 m) of 26-gauge wire	Measuring tape
32 rose montées (4 mm)	Wire cutters or flush cutters
20 bicones (3 mm)	Electrical tape
10 bicones (4 mm)	Square kumihimo disk
2 ribbon ends (8 mm)	2 pairs of chain-nose and flat-nose pliers
2 jump rings (5 mm)	E6000 glue
2 earring findings	

1 Cut sixteen 12" (30.5 cm) lengths of 26-gauge wire. Tape the wires together near one end.

2 Insert the taped end through the hole in the disk and hold it closely underneath. Attach the wires to the disk according to the Half-Round Kumihimo structure in Braid Structures, noting that two wires will be placed into each slot and treated as a single group. Create four rounds of the half-round braid.

3 To start round 5, move the wires from top slot 7 to left slot D and the wires from top slot 6 to right slot D **(FIGURE 1)**. Release the group of two wires in bottom slot 7, and separate them so they are positioned left and right of each other. Move this left wire to left slot A, while leaving the right wire stationary for now **(FIGURE 2)**. In the same manner, separate the group of two wires in bottom slot 6, and move the right wire to right slot A, leaving the left wire stationary **(FIGURE 3)**.

4 Pick up a rose montée, and notice the dual hole position is in a cross pattern on the back. Put one length of the stationary wire through one hole in a rose montée, and then put the other length of wire through the other hole, making sure the crystal is facing towards you

(FIGURE 4). Pull the wires to bring the montée down to the base of the braid, making sure it sits on the front of the braid. Reunite each of these wires with their original partner by placing them into the side A slots on the left and right side of the disk. **(FIGURE 5)**. Complete this round of the braid following the Half-Round Kumihimo structure (see steps 5–7 of the Half-Round Kumihimo structure instructions in Braid Structures).

5 Start the next round of the braid, except after releasing the wires from right slot C, add a bicone onto both lengths of wire **(FIGURE 6)** and slide it down between the wires going out to right slot A and D before proceeding to moving the wires to top slot 7 **(FIGURE 7)**. Finish this round following the normal braid structure.

NOTE | IF THE HOLE OF THE BICONE IS TOO SMALL FOR BOTH WIRES TO GO THROUGH, PUT ONE WIRE THROUGH THE HOLE AND RUN THE OTHER WIRE ALONG THE SIDE OF THE BEAD NEXT TO THE BRAID.

6 Continue braiding the wire, alternating between adding a rose montée and a bicone in every round. To graduate the size of the bicones on the braid: Add 16 rose

montées to the middle of the braid and the bicones to the edge in the following order: five 3 mm bicones, five 4 mm bicones, and five 3 mm bicones.

NOTE | WHEN MOVING THE BOTTOM GROUPS OF WIRES, MAKE SURE THEY GO AROUND THE SIDES OF THE PREVIOUSLY PLACED ROSE MONTÉES.

7 Complete the braid with four rounds of wire without adding in any beads. The braid coming out from underneath the disk will have a slight curve to it. This is normal.

8 Remove the braid from the disk. With the rose montées facing you, shape the braid using the existing curve by pushing the ends toward each other until they overlap at the top **(FIGURE 8)**.

9 Cut across both ends of the braid where they overlap with wire cutters to get a straight edge. Attach a ribbon end with glue over both ends of the braid, then use a jump ring to add an earring finding.

10 Repeat steps 1–9 to make the second earring.

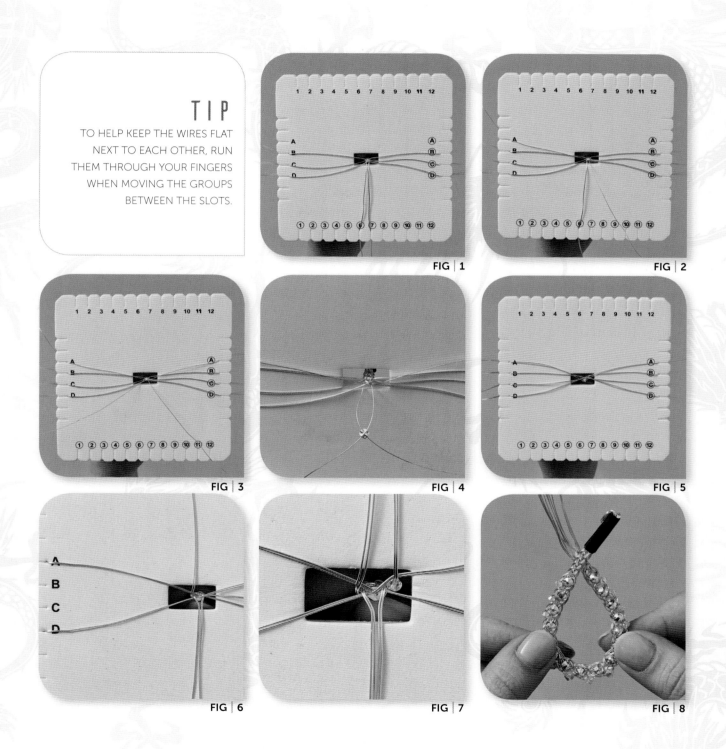

FIG | 1

FIG | 2

FIG | 3

FIG | 4

FIG | 5

FIG | 6

FIG | 7

FIG | 8

LEATHER
AND
WIRE

KUMIHIMO

This final section has projects that combine leather and wire in one piece. Incorporating leather into wire kumihimo adds another dimension to the jewelry and can create a completely different look. In some projects, leather is incorporated into the braid, while in others it is added as a feature after the braid has been made with wire. These designs are just the beginning of endless possibilities for combining leather with wire kumihimo.

CHEVRON

BRACELET

This was my first leather and wire kumihimo design. I had the idea of combining lengths of leather with thinner lengths of wire in one braid to create a different texture than couldn't be achieved by using either of the materials on their own. The texture had a chevron effect due to the braid structure, hence the name. This piece uses the basic Cross Kumihimo structure and is an easier project to make once you're familiar with that braid structure. The main things to pay attention to are setting up the lengths on the disk to achieve the desired effect and how to work with leather and wire within the same braid.

FINISHED SIZE | ⅜" × 8" (1 cm × 20.5 cm)　**LEVEL** | Beginner

---

MATERIALS

21⅓' (6.5 m) of 26-gauge wire

5⅓' (1.7 m) of 1 mm leather cord

2 ribbon ends (13 mm)

3 jump rings (5 mm)

1 lobster claw clasp

Extender chain

TOOLS

Measuring tape

Wire cutters or flush cutters

Scissors

Electrical tape

Square kumihimo disk

2 pairs of flat-nose and chain-nose pliers

E6000 glue

with your fingers as you move them to help the wires lay flat next to each other **(FIGURE 4)**. This gives the final piece a smoother look as the wires won't be crossing over each other too much.

4 Move the leather cord from top slot 5 to bottom slot 6. Then move the wires from bottom slot 5 to top slot 5 **(FIGURE 5)**. Repeat these steps on the other side of the disk in the mirror image: Move the wire from the bottom slot 7 to the top slot 7, top slot 8 to bottom slot 7, and bottom slot 8 to top slot 8 **(FIGURE 6)**.

5 Bring the cord from left slot B to bottom slot 5, then move the cord in right slot B into bottom slot 8 **(FIGURE 7)**. All the lengths are now in the original setup, but the groups of wire and the lengths of leather cord have swapped position on the disk. This will keep happening after every round of this braid structure.

6 Continue repeating steps 3–5 until the lengths of cord and wire have been braided. Remove the braid from the disk, holding the end so the leather doesn't unravel. To help secure the end, apply a few drops of glue on each end of the braid and around the area you plan to trim. Let the glue dry, then cut through the middle of the glued section with wire cutters, so it helps hold the end together while you attach the ribbon ends. Use jump rings to attach a clasp and extender chain to each end, and shape the bracelet as desired.

1 Cut sixteen 16" (40.5 cm) lengths of 26-gauge wire and four 16" (40.5 cm) lengths of 1 mm leather cord. Cut a 2" (5 cm) piece of electrical tape, and place it on your work surface, sticky-side up. Lay one end of a length of leather on the edge of the tape, and then arrange four lengths of wire beside it. Add another length of leather, then another group of four wires. Add the rest of the lengths in reverse order, starting with four lengths of wire and finishing with the final length of leather. Tape all the ends together, keeping the wires and cord flat next to each other **(FIGURE 1)**.

2 Insert the taped end through the hole in the disk, and hold it tightly just underneath. Attach the lengths to your kumihimo disk using the Cross Kumihimo structure in Braid Structures with the leather cords in slots 5–8 on the top of the disk and the groups of four wires in slots 5–8 on the bottom **(FIGURE 2)**.

3 Following the Cross Kumihimo structure instructions, move the leather cord in top slot 7 to left slot B and the cord in top slot 6 to right slot B **(FIGURE 3)**. Bring the group of wires in bottom slot 6 to top slot 6, making sure to move all four wires together as if they were one length and smoothing the wires

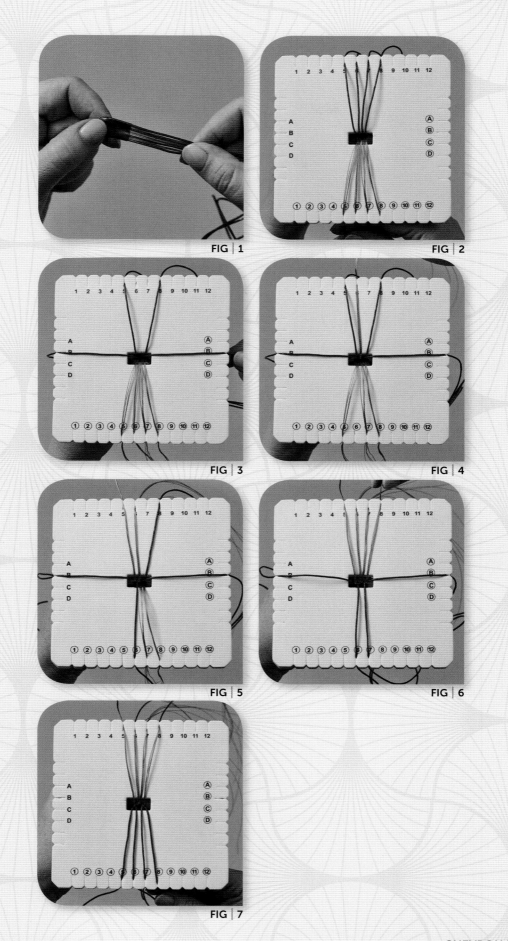

FIG | 1

FIG | 2

FIG | 3

FIG | 4

FIG | 5

FIG | 6

FIG | 7

CORSET
BRACELET

In this design, we use a basic braid structure, then add leather cord for a corset effect. You can create interesting combinations by mixing up the colors for both the wire and the leather cord. Just be sure to use an even tension while making the braid so you end up with an even corset effect.

FINISHED SIZE | ⁹⁄₁₆" × 8³⁄₈" (1.5 cm × 21.5 cm)   **LEVEL** | Intermediate

MATERIALS

16' (4.9 m) of 22-gauge wire

4¾' (1.5 m) of 0.5 mm leather cord

2 ribbon ends (20 mm)

3 jump rings (5 mm)

1 lobster claw clasp

Extender chain

TOOLS

Measuring tape

Wire cutters or flush cutters

Electrical tape

Square kumihimo disk

Scissors

Fine round-nose pliers

2 pairs of chain-nose and flat-nose pliers

E6000 glue

1 Cut eight 24" (61 cm) lengths of 22-gauge wire. Tape the wires together near one end.

2 Insert the taped end through the hole in the disk and hold it tightly just underneath. Arrange the wires on the disk according to the Diagonal Braid structure in Braid Structures. Make a 14" (35.5 cm) braid.

3 Remove the braid from the disk. Trim the ends, then cut the braid in half, so you have two 7" (18 cm) lengths.

4 Cut 27" (68.5 cm) of leather cord with an angle at each end to help thread the cord through the loops in the braid.

5 Lay both lengths of braid front-side up vertically next to each other on your work surface. Working from the bottom of the braids, thread one end of the cord through the first loop on the inner edge of the right braid from underneath and the other end through the first loop on the inner edge of the left braid from underneath. Pull the cord tight through both loops so the leather is evenly positioned between the braids, leaving a ¼" (6 mm) space between the two braids (FIGURE 1).

6 Skip the next two loops on the inner edge of the braid, then expand the third hole with fine round-nose pliers (FIGURE 2).

7 Thread the left side of the cord through the expanded loop on the right braid from below, and pull it tight (FIGURE 3). Bring the other side of the cord through the corresponding loop on the left braid from below. Pull the cord ends tight, so they form an X between the braids (FIGURE 4).

8 Continue working as in steps 6 and 7 to thread the cord through the braids, making sure to start with the left side of the cord each time until you reach the end of the braid.

9 Secure the ends of the cord by tying an overhand knot (FIGURE 5). Tighten the knot so it nestles in between the braids. Then tie a second knot for extra security (FIGURE 6). Trim the excess cords right after the knot.

10 Cut two 15" (38 cm) pieces of 0.5 mm leather cord. Expand the first loop on the outer edge of one of the braids using fine round-nose pliers (FIGURE 7). Thread one end of the cord through the loop from top to bottom, leaving a ½" (1.3 cm) tail. Expand the next loop on the outer edge of the braid and thread the cord from the top through this loop. Make sure to follow the direction of the braid structure so the cord nestles into the ridge between the loops, then pull the cord tight (FIGURE 8). Continue threading the cord through the next loop in the same direction until you reach the other end. Trim the excess cord on each end to the same length as the wire braids, so it doesn't unravel but is short enough to be captured inside the ribbon end. Thread the second cord on the outer edge of the other braid, and work in the same manner to add a cord to this side.

11 Finish the ends of the bracelet with the ribbon ends, capturing the leather cords inside (FIGURE 9). Attach the clasp and extender chain to the ribbon ends with jump rings, and shape the bracelet so it's ready to wear.

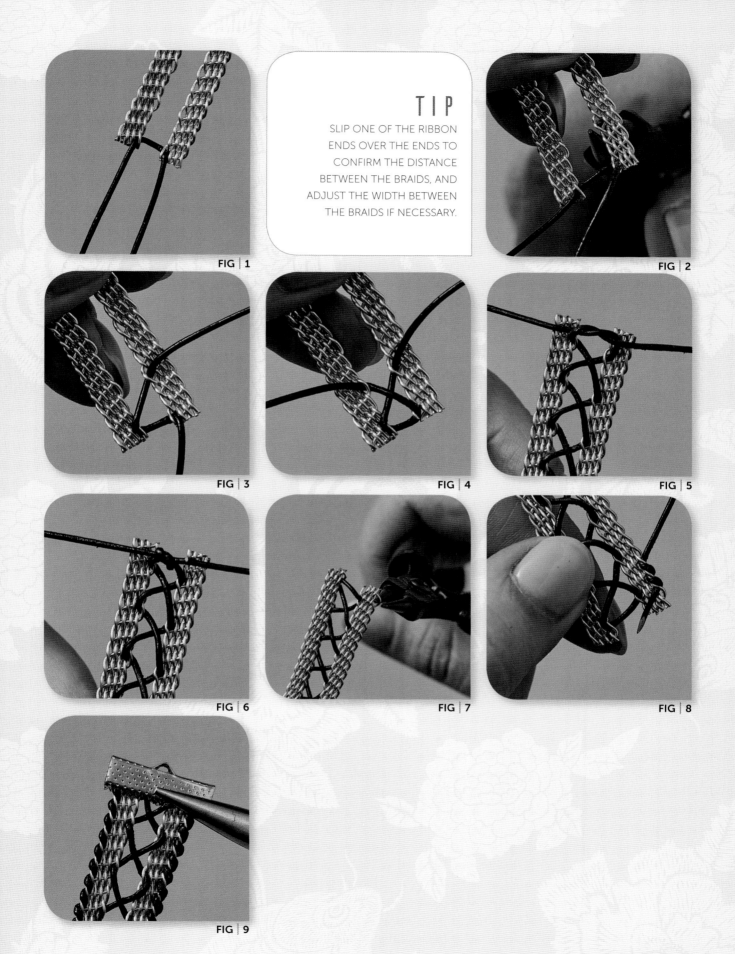

FIG | 1

TIP

SLIP ONE OF THE RIBBON
ENDS OVER THE ENDS TO
CONFIRM THE DISTANCE
BETWEEN THE BRAIDS, AND
ADJUST THE WIDTH BETWEEN
THE BRAIDS IF NECESSARY.

FIG | 2

FIG | 3

FIG | 4

FIG | 5

FIG | 6

FIG | 7

FIG | 8

FIG | 9

CORSET

EARRINGS

This pair of leather and wire kumihimo earrings is similiar to the Corset Kumihimo bracelet. Here, leather is added to a basic braid to achieve the corset effect. Leather comes in different hues, so you can customize the look of these earrings simply by changing the colors of the materials used.

FINISHED SIZE | 1³⁄₁₆" × 2½" (3 cm × 6.5 cm)   **LEVEL** | Intermediate

MATERIALS

18²⁄₃' (5.7 m) of 22-gauge wire

5⅚' (1.8 m) of 0.5 mm leather cord

2 ribbon ends (10 mm)

2 jump rings (5 mm)

2 earring findings

TOOLS

Measuring tape

Wire cutters or flush cutters

Electrical tape

Square kumihimo disk

2 mm mandrel

Fine round-nose pliers

Scissors

2 pairs of chain-nose and flat-nose pliers

E6000 glue

1 Cut eight 14" (35.5 cm) lengths of 22-gauge wire. Tape the wires together near one end.

2 Insert the taped end through the hole in the disk and hold it tightly just underneath. Attach the wires to the disk following the Diagonal Kumihimo structure in Braid Structures. Make a 6" (15 cm) diagonal braid.

TIP

IT IS IMPORTANT TO HAVE AN EVEN TENSION WHILE MAKING THE BRAID, SO IT ENDS UP BEING AS SYMMETRICAL AS POSSIBLE WHEN SHAPED.

3 Remove the braid from the disk, and leave the ends untrimmed for now. Place a small mandrel (about 2 mm) just to one side of the middle of the braid. With your thumb on the opposite side, start shaping the braid around the mandrel to create a V shape (FIGURE 1).

4 Using your fingers and working on one side at a time, make a slight curve evenly on each side of the braid to create a marquise shape with the braid ends overlapping (FIGURE 2).

5 With the front of the braid facing forward, slightly expand a loop on each side of the inner edge of the braid near the bend with a pair of fine round-nose pliers so the leather can easily fit through (FIGURE 3).

6 Cut a 20" (51 cm) length of 0.5 mm leather cord, trimming the ends at an angle. Thread one end of the cord through one of the expanded loops from the back (FIGURE 4), so the cord comes out toward the front. Using your fingers or chain-nose pliers, pull the cord through halfway, then put the other end through the corresponding loop on the opposite side (FIGURE 5). If the leather curls up on itself while threading it through the loop, undo the curling and keep pulling the leather until there is no excess on the back and the lengths are even.

7 Expand the next loop up on each inner edge, move the left cord diagonally over to the right side, and thread it through the widened loop from back to front. Pull the cord tight (FIGURE 6). Move the right cord diagonally and thread it through the widened loop on the left side from back to front, pulling it tight to form an X in the lower point (FIGURE 7).

8 Skip one loop, then enlarge the second loop on each inner edge with fine round-nose pliers. Thread the left cord through the expanded right loop from the back, pulling the cord tight. Then bring the right cord through the left loop from the back and pull the cord tight. Continue repeating this step and work toward the top point, making sure to start with the same side every time and skipping a loop on the inner edge of the braid. When the top is reached, skip trimming the cord ends for now.

9 Cut 15" (38 cm) of 0.5 mm leather cord, making sure to cut the ends at an angle. Starting on one side of the piece at the top, expand the first loop on one outer edge with fine round-nose pliers (FIGURE 8). Thread one end of the cord through the loop from top to bottom, leaving a 1" (2.5 cm) tail (FIGURE 9). Expand the next loop on the outer edge, and thread the cord from the top through this loop. Make sure to follow the direction of the braid structure so the cord nestles into the ridge between the loops, and then pull the cord tight (FIGURE 10). Continue widening and going through each loop on the outer edge until you reach the other end of the braid.

10 Using wire cutters, cut straight across both braids at the top where they overlap to achieve a flat edge (FIGURE 11). Cut the inner corners of the braid ends, if necessary to get a proper fit with the ribbon end.

11 Trim the excess leather cords, leaving a short tail so they don't unravel and can be captured inside the ribbon end. Add glue to the ends, clamp your ribbon end down on the end with flat-nose pliers, and attach the earring finding.

12 Repeat steps 1–11 to make the second earring.

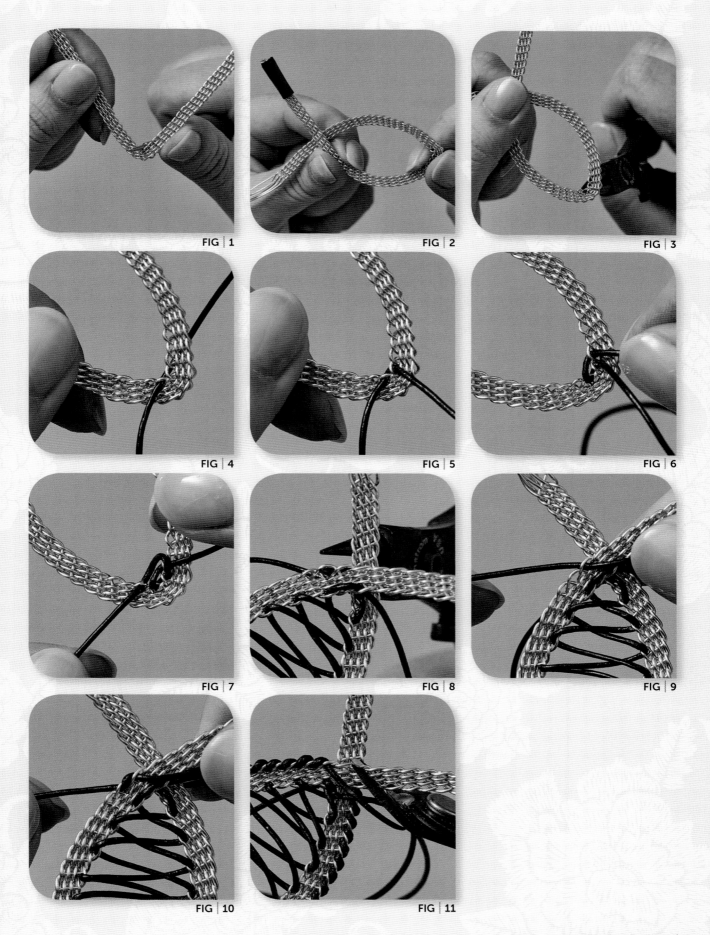

FIG | 1

FIG | 2

FIG | 3

FIG | 4

FIG | 5

FIG | 6

FIG | 7

FIG | 8

FIG | 9

FIG | 10

FIG | 11

FRAMED LEATHER

BRACELET

I was inspired to make a bracelet incorporating leather and wire by making multiple braids and combining them together in one piece. I thought one braid could incorporate the leather as a focal piece and be framed by wire braids to make it stand out. This bracelet uses the braid structures in a simple way, but results in a piece that looks more intricate than it actually is.

FINISHED SIZE | ⅜" × 8" (1 cm × 20.5 cm)   **LEVEL** | Intermediate

MATERIALS

11' (3.4 m) of 20-gauge wire

21⅓' (6.5 m) of 26-gauge wire

6' (1.9 m) of 1 mm leather cord

2 ribbon ends (20 mm)

3 jump rings (5 mm)

1 lobster claw clasp

Extender chain

TOOLS

Measuring tape

Wire cutters or flush cutters

Electrical tape

Square kumihimo disk

Scissors

2 pairs of flat-nose and chain-nose pliers

E6000 glue

1 Cut six 22" (56 cm) lengths of 20-gauge wire, and tape them together near one end.

2 Attach the wires to the disk by placing the two middle wires in top slots 6 and 7, the next wire on either side in slots 6 and 7 on the bottom, and the two remaining lengths in top slots 5 and 8 **(FIGURE 1)**.

3 Follow the structure for the Cross Kumihimo (see Braid Structures) by moving the wire in top slot 7 to left slot B and the wire in top slot 6 into right slot B. Move the wire from bottom slot 6 to top slot 6, then move the wire from top slot 5 to bottom slot 6. Move the wire from bottom slot 7 to top slot 7, then move the wire from top slot 8 to bottom slot 7. Bring the wires on the side of the disk back into the braid, by moving the wire from left slot B to top slot 5 and the wire from right slot B to top slot 8. The wires are now back in the original setup.

4 Repeat step 3 until all the lengths of wire are used up, then remove the braid from the disk. The braid should measure approximately 15-16" (38-40.5 cm).

5 For the second braid, cut sixteen 16" (40.5 cm) lengths of 26-gauge wire and four 18" (45.5 cm) lengths of 1 mm leather cord. Arrange the lengths in groups in this order: one leather cord, four lengths of wire, one leather cord, and then a group of four wires. Place the remaining lengths in the opposite order, so you end up with two four-wire groups in the middle right next to each other. Tape all the lengths together near one end **(FIGURE 2)**.

6 Insert the taped end through the hole in the disk and hold it tightly just underneath. Place the lengths on your disk according to the Half-Round Kumihimo structure in Braid Structures. Locate the two middle leather cords in the group, and place one in top slot 6 and one in top slot 7, then place the far left leather cord in left slot C and the far right leather cord in right slot C. Place the middle two groups of wires consisting of four lengths each in bottom slots 6 and 7, the left group of wires in left slot B and the last remaining group in right slot B **(FIGURE 3)**.

7 Move the leather cord in top slot 7 to left slot D and the leather cord in top slot 6 to right slot D **(FIGURE 4)**. Move the wires in bottom slot 7 to left slot A and the wires in bottom slot 6 to right slot A **(FIGURE 5)**.

8 Move the cord from left slot C to top slot 6, then move the wires from left slot B to bottom slot 6. Repeat these steps on the other side of the disk in a mirrored image by moving the cord from right slot C to top slot 7 and the wires from right slot B to bottom slot 7 **(FIGURE 6)**. Close the gap on the sides of the disk by moving the

wires from slot A on each side to slot B and the cord in slot D on each side to slot C **(FIGURE 7)**. All the lengths are now back in the original position.

9 Repeat steps 7–8 until all the lengths are used up. Carefully remove the finished braid from the disk by holding onto the end while releasing the cords and wires to prevent the braid from coming undone. Use some of the remaining lengths of wire to wrap around the end of the braid to temporarily secure the end of the braid to prevent it from unraveling.

10 Measure the desired length needed for the final braid (take the length of the clasp into account). Using wire cutters, cut the wire-only Cross Kumihimo into two even lengths. Then cut the half-round leather and wire braid to the same length as the Cross Kumihimo pieces. On your work surface, arrange the half-round leather and wire braid in the middle with one length of the wire-only braid on each side. Add a ribbon end, making sure to capture all three braid ends, on each end of the braids **(FIGURE 8)**. Use jump rings to attach a clasp and extender chain, and shape the bracelet (see Shaping a Bracelet in Finishing Kumihimo).

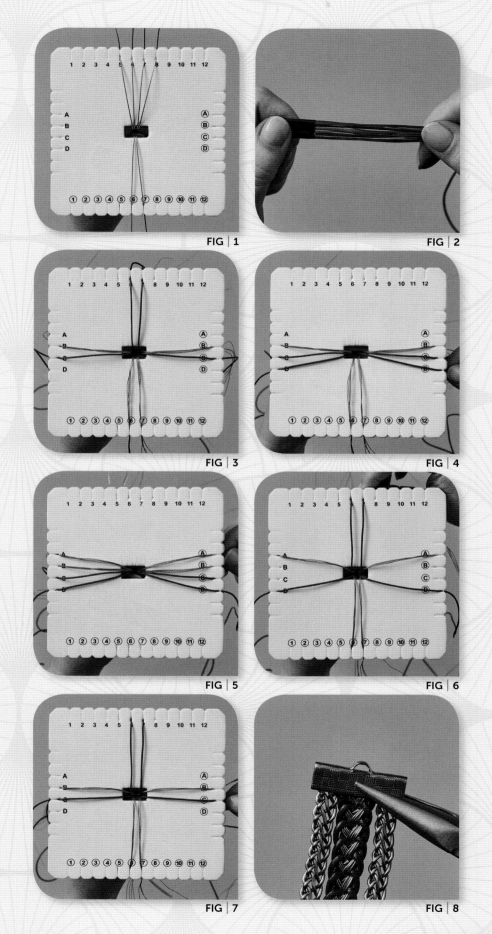

FIG | 1

FIG | 2

FIG | 3

FIG | 4

FIG | 5

FIG | 6

FIG | 7

FIG | 8

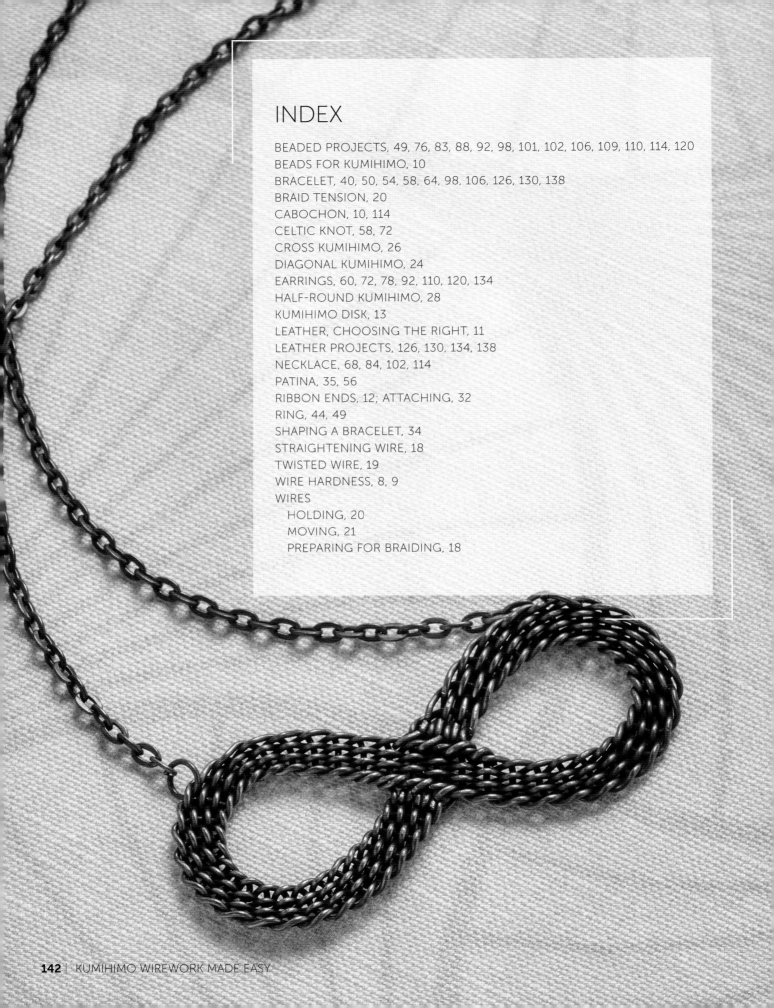

INDEX

ACKNOWLEDGMENTS

The opportunity to write this book has fulfilled a long-time dream, and I very much appreciate the trust that has been put into my work. The book came along when I was going through a difficult time, and working on this project helped me get to a better place. For that, I am grateful. The designs I created for this book may not have happened if it weren't for this opportunity. And writing this book got my creativity flowing like never before. I have immensely enjoyed the process, and I have to thank my other half for putting up with me and my work during it. I'm sure it can't have been easy, but I am very grateful to have such a supportive partner. I also want to acknowledge my mum, who helped nuture my creativity over the years. There wasn't one craft we didn't do together, and I appreciate the support and openness that has always been offered by her and my family. Lastly I would like to thank the editorial team, who helped guide me through writing this first book and bounced around great ideas for valuable content. The final book is definitely better for it.

ABOUT THE AUTHOR

Christina Larsen is a self-taught jewelry maker who designs jewelry within several different mediums, but kumihimo is one of her favorites. She loves to experiment with new techniques and materials, which is one reason she is so attracted to kumihimo—it has many possibilities. Kumihimo is also a very therapeutic medium, as the process of braiding is very repetitive. She creates tutorials for many of her designs on her popular Youtube channel, which has had millions of views, and aims to make her tutorials as easy to follow as possible for anyone who wants to learn.

Inches	Centimeters	2.54
Centimeters	Inches	0.4
Feet	Centimeters	30.5
Centimeters	Feet	0.03
Yards	Meters	0.9
Meters	Yards	1.1

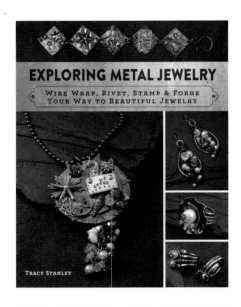
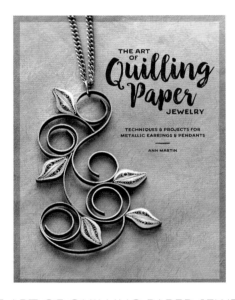